THE NEW
NATIVE AMERICAN
CUISINE

FIVE-STAR RECIPES FROM THE CHEFS OF ARIZONA'S KAI RESTAURANT

Marian Betancourt

with Executive Chef Michael O'Dowd and Chef de Cuisine Jack Strong
of Kai Restaurant at Sheraton Wild Horse Pass Resort & Spa
Food photography by Ron Manville

The Nation's First and Only AAA Five Diamond and Mobil Five Star Native American Restaurant
The Only AAA Five Diamond and Mobil Five Star Restaurant in Arizona

ThreeForks®

GUILFORD, CONNECTICUT
HELENA, MONTANA
AN IMPRINT OF THE GLOBE PEQUOT PRESS

A ThreeForks Book
ThreeForks is a registered trademark of The Globe Pequot Press.

Text design by Sheryl P. Kober. Layout by Melissa Evarts

Photo credits: pp. 25, 27, 37, 39, 48, 51, 54, 56, 61, 68, 71, 75, 87, 93, 97, 100, and 101 © Ron Manville; all others courtesy of Sheraton Wild Horse Pass Resort & Spa

Library of Congress Cataloging-in-Publication Data

Betancourt, Marian.
The new Native American cuisine : five-star recipes from the chefs of Arizona's Kai Restaurant /
Marian Betancourt ; with Michael O'Dowd and Jack Strong of Kai Restaurant at Sheraton Wild Horse
Pass Resort & Spa ; food photography by Ron Manville.
p. cm.
Includes index.
ISBN 978-0-7627-4895-2
1. Indians of North America—Food. 2. Indian cookery. 3. Cookery—Arizona. 4. Kai Restaurant
(Gila River Indian Reservation, Ariz.) I. O'Dowd, Michael. II. Strong, Jack, 1975- III. Title.
E98.F7B45 2009
641.59791—dc22
2009006981

Printed in China
10 9 8 7 6 5 4 3 2

In memory of my mother Dyna Maria Betancourt, who introduced me to the
magical Sonoran Desert at a very young age.
—M.B.

To my wife Linda, my sons Brandon and Rion, and my daughter Audrey, who have
been my culinary inspiration and who supported me through the years.
—M. O'D.

For my late mother Rowenda Strong, who is always with me,
and for my grandmother Wilma Strong, for her loving support.
—J.S.

Sheraton Wild Horse Pass Resort & Spa

CONTENTS

CONTENTS

INTRODUCTION

The *new* American cuisine for the world's foodies may very well be *Native* American cuisine if the chefs at the Kai restaurant at Sheraton Wild Horse Pass Resort & Spa have anything to say about it. At this cutting-edge restaurant on the edge of Phoenix—the only Native American restaurant in the nation to achieve AAA's Five-Diamond and Mobil's Five-Star status—the chefs bring an ancient cuisine into the modern spotlight with classical European culinary techniques, artful plating, and pairings with the finest wines. Grilled elk chop served with truffles provides a whole new taste experience. Try a sweet corn pana cotta with venison carpaccio. There's buffalo tartare with prairie quail egg, and butter-basted lobster with fry bread and avocado mousse. Goat's milk cheesecake on a base of mesquite meal or phyllo dough made with saguaro seeds are new to the palate, not to mention a blue cornmeal scone.

The New Native American Cuisine offers these exciting recipes and more, for small plates and main courses; soups and salads, fish, meat, game, vegetables, and desserts. Some of the recipes are complex, some simple, but all should appeal to those who want to add a new dimension to their culinary experience. A glossary explains the Native American terms, and a shopping guide helps you find comparable ingredients as well as such delicacies as saguaro blossom syrup, *cholla* buds, and tepary beans. Most of the ingredients for these recipes are available everywhere, and others can be easily acquired from specialty producers and online sources.

For a true appreciation of Native American cuisine, one must also understand the land and culture that gave rise to these simple flavors. Thus this book is not only a cookbook, it is also a guide to the rich history and culture of the farmers and ranchers of the Gila River Indian Community. Long before modern irrigation systems, the prehistoric tribes of the Sonoran Desert of southwest Arizona had figured out how to bring water to their crops. In fact, the name *Arizona* comes from a Pima word meaning "waters." This agricultural oasis around the Gila River that once kept the indigenous people healthy and prosperous is blooming again with citrus, melons, corn, beans, squash, eggplant, baby lettuces, peppers, and edible desert plants.

In addition to being great farmers, the people of the Gila River were great hosts; nothing could be more fitting than experiencing that hospitality where it originated. When you dine at Kai at the Sheraton Wild Horse Pass, you not only enjoy fine cuisine, you are at the source, where, from your table, you can still see wild horses, the ancient saguaro, and the gorgeous desert landscape.

The Sonoran Desert has been sustaining native populations with a highly nutritious diet of fruits and vegetables for thousands of years. All forms of nature, plants, animals, and birds, are revered as a meaningful part of the lives of the Pima and Maricopa.

CHAPTER 1

Celebrating the Bounty of the Sonoran Desert

*F*rom the terrace of Kai restaurant at the Sheraton Wild Horse Pass Resort & Spa, you can look out onto the great expanse of desert toward the Estrella Mountains, which the native people call Komatke, "home of the wind." Sometimes you catch a glimpse of the wild horses; perhaps a distant puff of dust as they run by, or, if you are particularly eagle-eyed, a white horse grazing in a mesquite thicket so crowded with plants, trees, and wildlife that the early people named it "New York" thicket. As many as 1,500 wild horses, descendants of the sturdy Spanish barb and other breeds, have roamed the lands of the Gila River Indian Community near Phoenix, Arizona, for more than 500 years. This is their home. It is also the heart of an agricultural heritage that flourished around the Gila River for thousands of years and inspired the Five Diamond dinners you enjoy at Kai.

In recent centuries, settlers and soldiers on the way to California came to depend on the generous and prosperous Pima and Maricopa people not only for food and fresh horses along their journey, but for their well-known hospitality. Their welcoming nature transformed what was believed to be hostile territory into a temporary sanctuary for those heading west. That tradition holds true today. This 2,400-acre luxury resort that provides the modern traveler with state-of-the-art accommodations and amenities is, most of all, a showcase of the heritage, culture, and art of the people who have lived here for thousands of years and created an agricultural oasis.

The hot, dry Arizona summer that sends most of us rushing into our air-conditioned homes is actually the time of year when native people planted corn, beans, squash, melons, and other food staples that flourished in the Sonoran Desert. They supplemented these crops with what was naturally available in the desert including game, mesquite beans, and cactus fruit such as cholla buds and saguaro syrup.

The People of the River

The first farmers of the desert Southwest were the Hohokam, predecessors of today's Pima, and the Maricopa. They reached a population of about half a million before they mysteriously vanished, leaving behind hundreds of miles of irrigation canals to produce thousands of acres of crops in the Gila River and Salt River area. In fact, the name Arizona comes from the Pima word *a'al-sho-shon*, meaning "many springs of water." Today the city of Phoenix uses these canals to provide water for its population, acknowledging the engineering expertise of the early native farmers.

Sometime in the mid- to late 1700s, the Pima welcomed into the Gila River Valley a migrating tribe from the southern Colorado River area that called itself Pee Posh (Maricopa), or "The People," who also trace their roots to the ancient Hohokam, meaning "those who have gone." (The Pima are also known as Akimel O'otham, which translates to "River People.") The two tribes became allies and farmers in the Gila River basin, placing great value on developing the land and utilizing water as a means to provide for community needs. Thanks to their irrigation system and water supply, they were better able to thrive than many other Indian settlements in the Southwest.

While the Pima and Maricopa have different languages, their similar cultural values are based on a sense of community sharing, helping each other for the common good. All forms of nature, plants, animals, and birds, are revered as a meaningful part of their lives. They consider the surrounding Estrella (Komatke) and South Mountain ranges to be sacred.

Archaeological evidence indicates that at least forty different plants were consumed by the early people including corn, beans, and squash as well as prickly pears, sunflower seeds, walnuts, acorns, pine nuts, and wolfberries. By analyzing remains at Hohokam sites, archaeologists also uncovered the importance of corn in the diet of the early people. The skeletons had teeth worn down by the grit the people had mixed with cornmeal during milling. And the bones of women's hands were well developed and strong, suggesting they used heavy stones to grind corn day after day.

The Gila River is Arizona's largest tributary to the Colorado River 500 miles downstream. It begins in western New Mexico in the Mogollan Mountain range and flows downstream across Arizona into Yuma at the southwestern corner of the state near the Gulf of California. This wide, continually flowing river, the source of the prosperity of native people, supported a heavy growth of cottonwood, willow, and arrow weed along its banks. For centuries rain and snowmelt from the mountains fed the Gila River's major tributaries: the Salt and San Francisco Rivers, Eagle Creek, Bonita Creek, San Simon Creek, and the San Carlos River.

George Webb, a Pima of the Gila River Indian Community who lived from 1893 to 1964, remembered the river as it was a century ago in his memoir, *A Pima Remembers Tucson*, first printed in 1959 and published by the University of Arizona Press in 1992.

"In the old days, on hot summer nights, a low mist would spread over the river and the sloughs. Then the sun would come up and the mist would disappear. On these hot nights the cattle often gathered along the river up to their knees in the cool mud. Soon some Pima boy would come along and dive into the big ditch and swim for awhile. Then he would get out and open the headgate and the water would come splashing into the laterals and flow out along the ditches. By this time all the Pimas were out in their fields with their shovels. They would fan out and lead the water to the alfalfa, along the corn rows, and over to the melons. The red wing blackbirds would sing in the trees and fly down to look for bugs along the ditches. Their song always means that there is water close by as they will not sing if there is not water splashing somewhere. The green of those Pima fields spread along the river for many miles in the old days when there was plenty of water."

The name Arizona comes from the Pima word *a'al-sho-shon*, meaning many springs of water.

The early people planted their fields by hand using sticks to make furrows for seeds, and later with plows drawn by horses. Whoever had the team helped those on other farms with the plowing, while they in turn offered other types of help such as distributing water to those who needed it. When an irrigation ditch needed cleaning, they went out together with their shovels to fix it. This community effort meant there were crops in every field so that from the top of any hill or mountain there was green along the river as far as the eye could see.

An Oasis in the Desert

With 3,500 native species of plants, the vast and beautiful Sonoran is the lushest desert in the world. The majestic saguaro cactus, with its arms upraised, is the most striking emblem of this desert.

The Sonoran Desert has been sustaining native populations with not only a highly nutritious diet of fruits and vegetables, but a flavorful one as well. While the basic diet relied on staples such as corn, beans, and squash, the native people learned which native plants added spice to dishes. Amaranth, for example, is used to flavor black bean cakes. Tiny berry-like pods of the chiltepin grew wild, its seeds scattered by birds. Many native tribes used this fiery spice to season their food. These chiles were so important to some tribes, such as the Papago (now Tohono O'odham), that they went on pilgrimages each year to gather the best and most abundant in the Sierra Madre range in Mexico.

From early spring to late autumn the native people harvested wild plants, berries such as juniper, strawberries, and raspberries, as well as piñon (pinyon pine) nuts, and walnuts. Desert cactus offer edible pods and bear fruit that is flavorful and juicy. The fruit of the saguaro was gathered by the women and made into syrup.

They extracted nourishment from the fruit of yucca, prickly pear, and cholla cactus.

Early people found sustenance from plants they could grow, irrigate, and harvest themselves, such as the culinary holy trinity to all native peoples of corn, squash, and beans, called "the three sisters."

Men prepared the ground and women usually followed behind to place the seeds in the furrows. While the men later gathered the crops from the fields, women carried the harvest home in huge baskets, which they made themselves. The women winnowed the grain by skillfully tossing it from flat baskets. They also did the grinding of the corn and prepared all of the food for cooking.

THE GREAT ARIZONA ICON

The tall, stately saguaro cactus, with its arms upraised, has become the icon of Arizona, a symbol widely depicted on pins and T-shirts in tourist shops and airport stores. It has lived in the Sonoran Desert for about 8,000 years and while always sacred to the native people, it is now sacred to everyone, protected by the state of Arizona, which named its blossom the state flower. In addition to being a "condominium" for Gila woodpeckers, which carve nests in the stems, and elf owls, which move in after the woodpeckers leave, the cactus was also an important source of food and shelter for the indigenous people of the desert. Flowers that bloom at night in April and May and close up by noon are followed in June by bright red, egg-sized fruit that tastes a bit like watermelon or fig. Many people still gather saguaro fruits as their ancestors have for hundreds of years, with long poles made of saguaro ribs. The New Year begins with the saguaro harvest that includes the fermentation of saguaro syrup to make a ceremonial wine used to herald the monsoon rains. Many natives of the desert still like to eat the juicy fruit raw or cook it down into sweet, nutritious syrup. The dried seeds, rich in proteins and fats, can be ground into flour. At Kai, saguaro syrup is used in several ways, including as a salad dressing for the tender greens grown by the children's farm. It takes this giant ten years to grow one inch, so when you see one forty or fifty feet tall it is probably a couple of hundred years old. When the saguaro arms begin to droop, it is a sign of old age, and when the cactus dies, its ribs are used for building fences and shade armadas.

THE VELCRO PLANT OF THE DESERT

The buds of the buckthorn cholla (pronounced "choya") cactus are picked in early spring and taste like a cross between an asparagus and an artichoke. Cholla plants can grow as tall as nine feet, and the buds were traditionally a source of protein for desert peoples. They are very high in calcium and very low on the glycemic index. Some cholla plants are fuzzy-looking and appear soft, but their sharp spines are painful to remove if they attach to you—thus, the nickname Velcro of the desert. Cholla buds need to be picked before they are fully open and cleaned by shaking them around in a jar of sand to remove the prickly spines. The buds are simmered in water until tender and drained. They have a viscous consistency like cooked okra, but are traditionally dried for use any time. That's how chefs at Kai get them so they are available year-round for dishes such as the mushroom and cholla bud accompaniment to tenderloin of buffalo.

For the Pima and Maricopa, like most of the Indian tribes in the Southwest, the mesquite bean was one of their most important and versatile foods. The beans were gathered in large quantities by the women, who then pounded them in mortars into a flour preserved for the winter.

In the valleys of the Gila River, the Hohokam hunted the plentiful jackrabbits and cottontails, and wild turkey, as steady sources of protein. The dry air and sunshine of the desert have always been an ideal means of preserving wild game. The women cut the meat into strips, seasoned it, and set it outside to dry. With beef, this became known as jerky and has evolved over the centuries into the popular *carne seca* ("dried meat") dish served in many restaurants in the area with the addition of sautéed onions and garlic and chiles. Tomatoes are usually added to make a savory filling for tacos, enchiladas, and deep-fried tortilla packets known as chimichangas.

Traditional Dwellings and Farms

Until the latter half of the nineteenth century, the most common dwellings of the native people were the *olas ki* and the *vatho*. The olas ki, or round house, was made from mesquite or cottonwood posts and willow. Slightly excavated, the brush-and-mud structure had a domed roof that was plastered with straw and mud to keep the rain out. This structure was used for shelter in cool weather. The only opening was a small door about two feet wide and four feet high. For countless generations they were built with natural materials found on the land and remained part of the landscape when the houses became vacant. The vatho was a four-posted arbor covered with saguaro cactus ribs and the long straight branches of the arrow weed shrub. This was where people cooked, ate, and slept during the warmer times of the year. These structures hold important cultural value as well as provide shelter. They represent a local custom passed down by our ancestors.

Everything that grew in the desert, and every part of everything that grew, was put to good use. Cattails, known as *ulvagi* by the Indians, are tall plants with roots that grow near riverbanks. The long, sturdy green leaves were woven into mats and also for roofing for their homes. The stalk was split and dried for basket weaving. The cattail head was a silky down used for stuffing pillows and insulating clothing. Even the fine yellow pollen, if gathered with great care, was mixed with water to make a sweet gruel or baked into a biscuit. (Today, plant pollens are widely used by chefs to garnish and flavor foods.)

The catclaw bush, or *oopat* in the Pima language, has a fragrant pink flower and sharp, curved thorns. These bushes were cut and dried for firewood. Sometimes they were piled high to serve as brush fences. Willow trees (*chuel*) grow to forty-five feet and can be found along streams throughout most of Arizona. Storage baskets were woven from wands of willow. The creosote bush, or *shegoi*, is also known as greasewood. This graceful shrub can grow to eleven feet, with small evergreen leaves and yellow flowers. Creosote has long been used as a medicine to treat pain, colds, and stomach aches.

Things Begin to Change

In the 1500s the Spanish, looking for cities of gold, claimed Arizona for their own and indeed, found gold in the Gila River, along with copper, which is abundant in this state. Using the river for trade for the next 200 years, the Spanish introduced several new plants such as wheat, chickpeas, lentils, lettuce, onions, leeks, garlic, anise, pepper, mustard, mint, melons, plums, pomegranates, and figs. They brought horses, sheep, pigs, goats, and cattle. In the 1700s their missionaries brought citrus trees to the Sonoran

THE THREE SISTERS

Corn, beans, and squash, the staples of Southwestern diet, are known as "the three sisters" because they support each other like a family. When planted together, the corn produces a sturdy stalk for the beans to climb. The beans, in turn, supply nitrogen to enrich the soil. Finally, the vines and leaves of the squash provide a ground cover to keep moisture in and weeds out. As a result, all three plants thrive.

Desert where they flourished because of the Gila River irrigation canals.

When the Spanish and the Mexicans came, a dynamic interchange of culinary cultures began. With the introduction of wheat, breads were more often made from flour than from the coarser cornmeal used in native breads. Wheat came to exceed corn in popularity, and today more wheat flour tortillas than corn tortillas are consumed in this part of Arizona. The newcomers also brought the chile, but it was not entirely new to the native people who had long been enjoying the fiery wild chiltepin of the desert.

After the Mexican-American War in the mid-1800s, the United States claimed Arizona as a territory and in 1859 created the Gila River Indian Community, the first reservation in Arizona. The effect was devastating to the native people.

The Loss of a Way of Life

As successful farmers, the Pima and Maricopa always had plenty of food to sustain their families and to trade with the Spanish, Mexicans, and

THE ALL-PURPOSE TREE

Mesquite trees (*kui*) are the all-purpose plant of the desert. The thorny tangles of these shrubs or low trees have small, delicate leaves, straight spines, and yellow flowers followed by bean pods. The trees themselves provide protection for animals and native grasslands. The wood is used for fence posts and as fuel. Mesquite branches also provide wonderful flavor to meat that is cooked over a fire of the branches. The edible bean pods once provided a source of food, but this is no longer true. Mesquite beans, harvested from September to November, have a sweet taste, like chocolate or caramel, and can be dried and made into flour or used as a flavoring in jelly. The Mesquite Bean Martini served at Kai is prepared with syrup made from the beans, and the beans themselves are used in salsas and other dishes. The black resin of the mesquite bark has been used to cure many ailments, and even as a shampoo and hair dye. It has long been used by the Maricopa to paint their pottery.

European settlers. But as more white settlers moved to the area and the United States government took over, that changed. The Gila River dried up as trappers hunted beaver to extinction along the river, and this contributed to more erosion of the watershed, as did the intensive farming by settlers who irrigated the lands from the river's water. And then the United States government built dams that diverted waters of the river and its tributaries, until by the early twentieth century the Gila River ran dry and the way of life of the native people was wiped out. In 1868 a private U.S. company began making new use of the centuries-old abandoned Hohokam irrigation ditches, and the town of Phoenix was born.

From an independent agrarian society harvesting the desert for all their needs, the Pima and Maricopa became dependent on government food handouts such as flour, lard, sugar, and canned goods. Today's most widely known native food, fry bread, does not come from native tradition but developed from necessity because of the white flour and lard rationed by the U.S. military to the tribes it displaced in the nineteenth century. However, these flat discs of deep-fried dough are quite beloved by the native people, and many take a competitive pride in how they make it. (You will find a recipe for Third-Generation Fry Bread in this book, along with some new ways to serve it, such as a base for Butter-Basted Lobster, or Kahlúa and Chocolate Ice Cream with Ancho-Caramel Sauce.)

Without their physically active occupation and natural diet of desert plants that release sugars slowly into the blood, as opposed to refined sugars and starches that metabolize quickly, the Pima and Maricopa developed diabetes that shortened their life spans. The native people had a history of longevity, attested to by three beautiful portraits, charcoal drawings by Russell Blackwater at the resort, which portray chiefs who lived more than 100 years. Chief Tashquent is the one with the dreadlocks (hair was worshiped). Chief Owl Ear is portrayed

The ceiling dome in the two-level lobby of the Sheraton Wild Horse Pass Resort & Spa is painted with ten mural panels of the Pima and Maricopa cultures. The 500 guest rooms are in two wings off the lobby.

showing off a calendar stick—a large wooden staff carved with special signs used to record tribal and family history. Chief Azul, the last chief before the diabetes epidemic, died in 2002 at age 109.

During the twentieth century the Pima became better known around the world for diabetes than for their culture and history, with more than half the people over thirty-five contracting the adult-onset form of the disease.

Four times as many Pima Indians die from the disease compared with whites and twice as many compared to blacks, although the entire population of the United States is now at the same risk because of the focus on refined and processed foods, and more sedentary lifestyles.

But the tide has turned, and the Pima and Maricopa are restoring their farms and once again producing the foods that once provided their healthy lifestyle.

Today Gila River Farms looks like a big green oasis interwoven with irrigation canals.

CHAPTER 2

Reclaiming an Agricultural Heritage

The Gila River will never flow as it once did, and the dams that diverted so much of its water will not come down. Wildlife and plant life that graced the riverbanks from the beginning of time have disappeared, changing the landscape of the early people's homeland. But the native people are getting their water back. A historic 2004 water settlement decreed by the U.S. Supreme Court returned the water to the community by way of the Pima-Maricopa Irrigation Project. When completed, there will be more than 2,400 miles of canals and pipeline to irrigate 146,330 acres of community land. This landmark settlement—the largest Indian water rights settlement in U.S. history—sets a precedent that tribal nations across the country can follow. The irrigation will permit the community to become self-sustaining as it once was.

The Great Citrus Harvest

When the Spanish missionaries brought citrus trees to the area in the 1700s, the trees adapted and thrived in the Gila River area irrigated by the native people. The citrus planted here uses less water than other varieties and, because of the particular microclimate, no flies bother the groves, so it is not necessary to use pesticides. Today, Gila River Farms looks like a big green oasis interwoven with irrigation canals. One

thousand acres of citrus trees—about 75 to 100 per acre—line up neatly in long rows to produce 102 varieties of super-juicy citrus including blood oranges, ruby red grapefruit, and Meyer lemons. Citrus is harvested from October to December and sold to cooperatives, which then sell it to stores and restaurants. At the Kai restaurant, many types of this citrus are used for cocktails, tangy salad dressings, and even to flavor the water served to diners.

Established in 1969, this vital farming enterprise for the Gila River Indian Community is composed of five ranches, with approximately 12,500 acres irrigated each crop year. Independent farmers cultivate an additional 22,000 acres of similar crops. Total agricultural product value is $25 million annually. In addition to citrus, Gila River Farms produces melons, onions, and small grains. Not only do the fruit and vegetables thrive, but Pima cotton has long been a mainstay of Arizona agriculture, and cotton fields with their bright yellow blooms are part of the local landscape.

The combination of long, sunny days and cool desert nights is also the ideal growing condition for olives. In this prime area, the farms grow classic olives from Italy and Spain. Unlike other olive growing regions, there are no problems here with the olive fly. The resulting olive oil has

THE FAMOUS PIMA COTTON

American Pima cotton is a fine, silky cotton that has been grown in Arizona since the early 1900s. During World War I, it was used to make the cords and high-quality fabrics to cover the fuselage and wings of new airplanes. It was christened Pima in recognition of the native people who were helping to raise this cotton on a U.S. Department of Agriculture experimental farm in Sacaton. For most of the twentieth century, Arizona was the nation's largest producer of this cotton until growers in California took the lead. At Kai, the cotton tradition is recognized in the cotton candy used in Wood-Grilled Squash Puree.

a delicate and lively flavor to rival the finest oils from Europe. In addition to tapenades, these olives are used at Kai to make Blue Corn Scones with Candied Olives, and Olive Oil Gelato.

The farms also provided pasture for cattle and sheep grazing during the winter months. One of the main goals of the farms is to promote healthy foods to the 18,000 people who are part of the Gila River Indian Community.

The Youngest Farmers

One of the most exciting aspects of this agricultural renaissance is that the elementary and middle school children of the Gila River Indian Community are at the forefront. The children of the Gila Crossing School learn how to garden, and they take some of their harvest home with them for the whole family to use. They are the ones introducing their elders to what was once a healthy diet. Although some of the older boys refuse to take home eggplant lest their friends make fun of them for preferring vegetables over the more "manly" meat, according to Tim Moore, the agriculture instructor, the little kids want to eat everything, even the weeds.

Moore, who is called Mr. Tim by the children, is himself one of eight children raised on a farm in Iowa. He recalled picking 300 pounds of strawberries with his mom in a day. Before joining the Gila Crossing program, he ran a small farmers' market in Tempe and managed gardening operations at The Farm at South Mountain in Phoenix. Protected from the sun by a wide-brimmed outback hat, he cut a prickly pear from a cactus and cut it up, releasing its bright red tart-sweet red juice, for a visitor to taste. When the prickly pears bloom, it is a sign that the monsoon rains will begin.

The school program took root in the 1990s, spurred by the community's concern with health issues. It is hoped that by growing their own vegetables, children will be encouraged to eat fresh produce and help ward off problems of obesity and diabetes. In tribal elementary schools, children learn basics of good nutrition and exercise as well as the risks and complications of diabetes. There is also a strong heart study aimed at preventing heart disease. Health educators go into the neighborhoods not only to talk, but to eat and exercise with the tribal families. In nine years, Moore said, his student population jumped from 65 to 480 pupils. With the help of a grant from the U.S. Department of Agriculture, the fifth grade is now learning propagation.

The children of the Gila Crossing School learn how to garden and they take some of their harvest home for the whole family to enjoy.

Cholla plants have sharp spines that are difficult to remove if they attach to you, thus the nickname, Velcro of the desert.

The elementary students have one-third of an acre plus an orchard to cultivate, while the middle school has a full acre and orchard, with plum, apple, peach, fig, and pomegranate trees. They also maintain a greenhouse for year-round cultivation of delicate greens and herbs. The garden is named Ve chij O'otham ees, which means "young people planting."

With gardening the children also learn tribal history and culture as well as the culture of their foods. They learn the Pima words for what they grow and how foods were traditionally prepared. They also learn the business side of agriculture and are encouraged to take an entrepreneurial attitude, developing skills for pricing, marketing, packaging, and going after investment capital. The children sell their produce directly to Kai, including hand-picked lettuces, herbs, eggplant, chiles, and pomegranates.

The Gila Crossing School children also maintain a garden at the Heard Museum in Phoenix (see Appendix B: Where to Learn More), and participate in the annual Indian Market there under the auspices of the museum's education department.

Conserving Historic Seeds

An important part of the restoration of this agricultural heritage is the preservation of native seeds that began here in 1983, at the request of the Tohono O'odham people (cousins of the Pima) near Tucson. They wished to grow traditional crops but could not locate seeds; as a result, Native Seeds/SEARCH (NS/S) was founded in Tucson to conserve, document, and distribute the adapted and diverse varieties of agricultural seeds and their wild relatives. SEARCH is an acronym for Southwestern Endangered Arid Regional Clearing House.

Nearly half the world's leading food crops can be traced to plants first domesticated by indigenous people, not only in Arizona's Gila River area, but all over the world. Europeans were introduced to a bountiful table of potatoes, peanuts, beans, tomatoes, and maize or corn, the most significant contribution. But since the 1500s, more than half these distinctive seeds and breeds that fed America have vanished.

About 2,000 different seeds of traditional crops used as food, fiber, and dye by the Native Americans of the Southwest are now in the Native Seeds/SEARCH seed bank. More than half are corn, beans, and squash, the famous "three sisters" of agriculture. Beans such as tepary and Rio Zape are used in a variety of dishes at Kai, including Wood-Grilled Squash Puree with Rio Zape Beans. The seed bank also has a variety of chiles, amaranth, Zuni tomatillo, Sonoran white wheat, melons, and the l'itoi onion, a delicious vegetable that looks like a scallion but has a wonderful, tangy flavor that can replace either chives or shallots in many dishes. The signature mole sauce was developed at Kai from chiles grown with native seeds.

This Native Seeds/SEARCH genetic library also helps ensure that future agriculture will be sustainable and environmentally safe. In addition to being drought tolerant, many desert crops are resistant to chemical stressors and insects. The seeds are distributed to traditional communities and to gardeners worldwide. Both the seeds and membership are free to Native Americans living in the Southwest.

Similar seed banks are under way in other parts of the world, especially arid lands. Today Native Seeds/SEARCH is part of a global movement to preserve the heritage foods. Many organizations, such as Slow Food USA, are involved in this effort, as well as chefs and

THE VERSATILE PRICKLY PEAR

The prickly pear is a wild, shrubby cactus with small, barbed needles on its flattened, rounded pads. Bright flowers are followed in the spring by an egg-shaped, fleshy fruit called *tunas*, technically a berry, that has a tart-sweet taste with a hint of watermelon. Prickly pear syrup, derived from boiling down the fruit, is a popular flavoring in jelly, candy, lemonade, and margaritas. Nopales or nopalitos are the pickled pads of the prickly pear cactus, and they taste a bit like green beans. The thorns in the pad must be removed by hand, a tedious job. Chefs at Kai also use the pads in relishes and garnish, and the syrup in a wide range of foods.

foodies. A worldwide coalition of experts on sustainable agriculture known as RAFT, for Renewing America's Food Traditions, aims to safeguard our food traditions not the way a museum would, but by celebrating them as parts of living culture. The plan is to integrate these foods into diets and local economies. In addition to Native Seeds/SEARCH and Slow Food USA, the group includes The American Livestock Breeds Conservancy, Center for Sustainable Environments, Chefs Collaborative, Cultural Conservancy, and the Seed Savers Exchange.

As many as 1,500 wild horses roam the lands of the Gila River Indian Community.

CHAPTER 3

Sheraton Wild Horse Pass Resort & Spa: A Showcase for the Story

"I like to say Starwood broke 117 rules to accommodate the community," said Ginger Sunbird Martin about the company that manages the resort through its Sheraton brand. Sunbird Martin, thirty-five, a Pima born and raised in the Gila River Indian Community and the oldest of seven children, is the resort's Cultural Concierge—the first such position in the nation.

A great deal of attention was paid to details when the resort was designed, because while the Gila River Indian Community people created the Wild Horse Pass Resort & Spa to build their economy—90 percent of the resort profits provide health care, education, police and fire protection, and programs for young people—more importantly, they wanted to tell their story.

The guiding spirit of the Pima and Maricopa is the sun, so the resort entry faces east to welcome it. "In designing the resort, the tribe wanted all doors facing east," said Sunbird Martin. "It was not possible for all doors to face east, so the tribe ensured that the main entrance doors face this direction." The dome shapes of the main lobby and the separate spa and golf club represent historic Pima dwellings, or olas

kis, the round structures made from arrow weed. The circular patterns visible throughout the resort depict the cycles of life and the connection of all living things to each other and to the land. A "new" Gila River flows through the resort, an artificial redirection of the river and a visible reminder that water is the source of life to the Pima and Maricopa people. A small boat ferries visitors between sites at the resort along the river.

Sunbird Martin, who graduated from Arizona State University with a degree in American Indian Studies specializing in water rights, provides cultural orientation to new staff, works with meeting planners to incorporate native culture into their events, and acts as liaison between the resort and tribe's Cultural Committee, which oversees all resort cultural representations from menu tastings, to uniforms, to the use of native names for new areas. For example, the Aji Spa takes its name from the Pima word for sanctuary. In times of conflict, O'otham women and children were sent to Aji, a safe haven in the hills of the Gila River Indian Community. The Whirlwind Golf Club pays homage to Komatke, the home of the wind, or Hevel Ki in Pima language. The land to the east of Komatke is a place where several whirlwinds can be seen. Another golf hole faces Vikam Gahkotkt, also known as the Superstition Mountain, just east of Phoenix. In the legend of the Great Flood in the Pima creation story, a medicine man sang songs on top of the Superstition Mountain. Each time he sang, the mountain would rise high above the rising floodwaters, allowing the people to climb higher to avoid drowning. After his fourth attempt to raise the mountain to the heavens to save the people, he realized his powers were not strong enough. Instead, he turned the people into stone. From a distance, this craggy monolithic mountain does look like a group of "stone people" or Hothai O'otham.

Storytelling and Song

As Cultural Concierge, Sunbird Martin helps tell the story of the Pima and Maricopa with guest tours that highlight the history and culture of the tribes that lived there for more than 2,300 years. She also created a Storytelling and Song program for guests that takes place each winter and has become one of the most popular events at the resort. Guests can gather around the fire pit off the lower lobby for an hour-long sharing of ancient Pima and Maricopa legends based on desert wildlife. Typically, the stories have a moral lesson, and there are also personal stories about their experiences growing up on the surrounding tribal lands. Storytellers, such as Tim Terry, are all members of the Gila River Indian Community.

The native people called talking "throwing words into the air." Although they had no written language based on an alphabet until the last century, they have long recorded their history on large wooden sticks made from pine or other wood. They called them calendar sticks and carved them with special signs that represent particular events. The notches and cuts record various happenings, which only the owner of the stick can interpret. The distance between the carved notches on the stick represents intervals of time, typically from one saguaro harvest to the next. The use of the calendar stick dates back to at least the seventeenth century, and only a few tribal members were interpreters. Many of the people recorded their history in this way, and sometimes in the evenings they gathered to hear the tribal historians read the sticks. They might relate a traditional story, or tell what had happened in their grandfather's time.

A Sophisticated Culture

Both tribes of the Gila River Indian Community have highly evolved artistic cultures. Pima are known for their basketry, using all natural materials, such as willow shoots, cattails, and devil's claw that must be carefully selected and collected at the proper time of the year.

Baskets served practical purposes for serving, sifting, and carrying. Some were lined with pitch to make them waterproof. Baskets are usually black and beige with a black center in the design. A whirlwind is one of the most popular patterns. Another is the "Man in the Maze" pattern representing an ancient life path that follows the course of Se'he, or the Creator. The maze represents life's journey, the search for physical, social, mental, and spiritual balance, and the choices people make. By tracing the path of the man at the entrance, you will find that there is a single path and that the path has no shortcuts. Nor are there any dead ends. The narrow channel near the end of the path represents the end of life, where a person who has followed the creator's instructions will reach the center and will be greeted by the sun god, who will help him pass into the next world with a special blessing.

One painting at the resort depicts a mating ritual called the basket dance. While women dance with their baskets, men pick a mate not by her looks or how well she dances, but for her basket design and weave. It is fun to look at all the designs and imagine how such choices were made depending upon what the man wanted from a wife. Is it an orderly pattern? Are there playful flourishes?

The Maricopa are potters known for their exquisite black geometric designs of animals and people in red (or buff) clay. Unlike other artifacts, pottery alters little over time, and much of what we know about ancient cultures is learned from examining the records left in fired clayware—one reason it is so coveted by collectors and museums. Much of this pottery was dug up and taken away for study to universities and museums. This practice naturally offended the Maricopa people, and today many of the unearthed artifacts are being returned to the people by those museums and universities.

Pottery is linked to the spiritual world and the artist's connection to the earth and to his or her ancestors. The Maricopa decorated their pottery with natural dyes such as black paint made from mesquite bark resin. The potter's wheel was never used in Maricopa clay work, and today's artists work by hand with the same methods passed down for centuries. Originally, simple jars and bowls were created for storage needs, and were made of natural materials found on the land. Later, the clay work became more decorative, with geometrical designs, animals, people, and special symbols depicted in natural dyes.

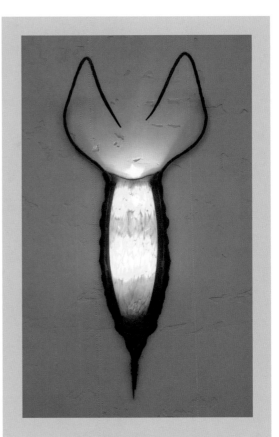

THE DEVIL'S CLAW

Visitors to the Wild Horse Pass Resort & Spa conference center are intrigued by the wall sconces fashioned in the shape of the devil's claw, or *ihuk* as the Pima say. They often mistake them for animal horns. The green pods of this plant were used as food, but more commonly, the pods, once dry and black, were used for basketry. This plant has shiny green leaves on trailing two- to five-foot-long stems. After seasonal rains it blooms with bright-colored flowers, and then it produces the dramatic claw-shaped seed pods. When soaked, these pods are pliable and strong.

Maricopa potters are known for their black geometric designs of animals and people in red or buff clay.

Every piece of art in the resort's collection is approved by a committee of elders from the Gila River Indian Community. In addition to pottery and baskets, there are paintings, drawings, photography, tile murals, ceremonial clothing, jewelry, textiles, calendar sticks, rasping sticks, hand-painted gourds, and flutes. All the contemporary artwork is done by people of the Gila River Indian Community. There's also a children's art gallery, including a striking depiction of wild horses.

The ceiling dome in the resort's two-level lobby is painted with ten mural panels, each showing a different aspect of the Pima and Maricopa culture: creation, elders, youth, games, Pima singers, hunting, Maricopa singers, basket weaving, pottery making, and gathering. The resort's 500 guest rooms are located in two wings off the central lobby—the Pima Wing and the Maricopa Wing. Each room is decorated with a sepia-toned historical photo of the desert landscape, as well as baskets in the Pima wing and pottery in the Maricopa wing. The restaurants, including Ko'Sin, which is open for all meals, and Kai, for dinner only, include many works of art reflecting the farming heritage of the Pima and Maricopa people.

A Home to Wild Horses

As many as 1,500 wild horses roam the lands of the Gila River Indian Community. When the Spanish brought horses to the Southwest more than three centuries ago, most Indian tribes gladly welcomed the new "technology," which allowed them greater mobility. The Pima and Maricopa quickly became accomplished horsemen and were caretakers of a sizable herd. Horses left behind by the Spanish sojourners flourished in the West and rapidly multiplied into vast herds.

Each spring, a large horse roundup was held near the great "New York" mesquite thicket mentioned in Chapter 1. In each village men would stand on top of a house and call the people to a meeting to discuss plans and set a date for the roundup. A smoke signal alerted the men that the drive was to begin, and the experienced riders drove the horses to a box canyon that served a corral at the foot of the Estrella Mountains (Komatke). They shouted and galloped their horses until they could no longer see one another because of the dust. The only sound was the thundering hooves.

Europeans and Mexicans and later American soldiers and settlers crossed the Gila River on the way to California and came to depend on the Pima and Maricopa for fresh horses along their journey. Military outfits often left their tired horses in the people's care and continued their journeys on new horses from local herds. Because of the continuous mix of new horses, the bloodline of this colorful herd now represents many hardy breeds.

Today this wild herd is under the protection of the Gila River Indian Community. Often, groups of horses can be seen grazing or gathering at watering holes near Wild Horse Pass. While visitors obviously cannot ride the wild horses, they can ride gentle horses at the resort's Koli Equestrian Center in the heart of the reservation.

A Walk through History

A two-and-a-half-mile interpretive trail at the resort follows alongside a replication of the Gila River. Here, with the aid of fifty detailed signs in English and the Pima language, you can learn more about the culture, history, and plant life of the Gila River Indian Community. More than half the signs focus on the vegetation that is of historical significance to the Pima and Maricopa people. Each sign features a picture of a plant and denotes what it was used for and its significance to the Gila River people. The remaining signs detail facts about the surrounding area such as the history of Pima cotton and the Pima and Maricopa languages. The construction of the trail took three years of in-depth research overseen by the Cultural Committee. Children enjoy taking guided tours of the trail with the resort staff.

A common visitor from the ancient past, walking freely and happily around the resort trails and grounds, is the roadrunner, known as the *tada* in Pima. Probably one of the most famous of the desert creatures because of its distinctive beep-beep sound and the Warner Brothers cartoon, this large black-and-white-mottled ground bird with a crested head is actually from the cuckoo family. Roadrunners would rather walk than fly and can move up to seventeen miles an hour along the desert floor. This bird only flies when it is running downhill or senses danger. It has short wings and big feet with two toes in front and two behind on each foot. This desert bird survives because, like the cactus plant, it hoards water in its body. The roadrunner has an oversized bill which makes it deadly to its primary prey—the rattlesnake. Because it is so quick, it is one of few animals able to catch a rattler. In fact, it uses its wings like a matador's cape, snaps the coiled snake by the tail, then cracks it like a whip against the ground until it dies.

According to Pima legend recalled by George Webb, a long time ago a woman had a pet rattlesnake (*koi*) and when it died she had no fire with which to cremate her pet. The roadrunner, offering to procure fire for her, flew up to the sun on a four-day-long journey. On his return trip a thunderstorm arose and lightning struck him right on the head, but he brought back the fire. That is how the roadrunner got red on his head.

Be assured there are no rattlesnakes at the Sheraton Wild Horse Pass Resort & Spa, and the roadrunners are perfectly happy with bugs and other small prey.

CHAPTER 4

Putting a New Spin on an Ancient Cuisine

Kai's unique cuisine was developed by Executive Chef Michael O'Dowd, who named it "Native American with Global Accents." Working from a triple-wide trailer before the restaurant was completed in 2002, O'Dowd began planning how this concept would be put into practice. He went into the Gila River Indian Community and asked people about their food and how they prepared it.

"They resisted the food inquiries," Sunbird Martin said. "'Why should we give our recipes to non-Indians?' they wanted to know." One of the challenges facing the chefs was to learn how to correctly prepare traditional bread such as chemaith and fry bread. Photos in the archives depict the elders in toques working with the chefs to resolve this problem. Sunbird Martin recalled that Native American Chef de Cuisine Jack Strong made the bread nine times before he got it right. Bread making in the native community is mostly an inherited skill with considerable pride attached, with many claiming, "My grandma makes it better than yours." However, "It's hard to make it just right. We had to learn to roll it with our hands, and it has to puff up properly. It is a delicate dough," recalled Chef Strong. The Third-Generation Fry Bread name comes from an early cook, Jesse Zillioux, who learned it from his mom who learned it from her

mom, thus the name. At Kai chemaith and other indigenous breads are served with dinner on a round, flat, clay-colored plate with an overlapping dish of locally grown olive oil that is pressed in nearby Queen Creek and served with a few seeds and nuts added. Fry bread is also used as part of a dish, such as lobster and ice cream.

Kai chefs worked closely with Gila River Farms and Gila Crossing elementary schools to plan how to incorporate locally grown and indigenous ingredients into the menu based on classical European techniques woven with traditional techniques of native elders.

Chefs at Kai buy squash, tepary beans, cow beans, and sixty-day corn, as well as Pima watermelon from the Tohono O'odham, who live farther south, between Tucson and Ajo. The Tohono O'odham are related to the Pima and are also restoring their agricultural heritage. Their name means "desert people," although for a long time they were known as Papago, a derisive name given them by the Spanish that means "tepary bean eaters." Some maps still list the Papago Reservation, but the Tohono O'odham changed that name long ago. Tohono O'odham Community Action (TOCA) is reintroducing the traditional desert-based foods.

The foods of other tribes are also included in the Kai menu, such as the Cheyenne River buffalo raised by the Sioux, and fish from tribes in the Northwest. A grass-fed grilled tenderloin of buffalo, for example, is served with cholla buds and wild mushrooms, along with squash blossoms from the children's farm and saguaro blossom syrup.

Welcome to Kai

In addition to being great farmers, the Pima and Maricopa tribes were great hosts. Early settlers traveling west, who may have feared hostility from the native people, found instead people who welcomed them and shared what they had. These two themes are the foundation of the resort and showcase the fine dining restaurant, Kai, which opened in 2002.

Located just off the resort's main lobby, Kai's spacious lounge encourages guests to relax in the comfortable leather armchairs in front of the fire and enjoy a pre-dinner martini of specialty vodkas featuring community-grown citrus, such as the Great Fruit Martini or the Mesquite Bean Martini.

Guests are greeted in the Pima language by the staff, which is under the leadership of O'Dowd and Strong. When spoken, "Good day, my name is David. How are you doing?" sounds like "Skuk tash aknee up chew geek David. Shop a mas a ma?"

The mostly young wait staff, dressed in black trousers and shirts, delivers each course to everyone at your table at the same time. This is part of the Pee Posh service, which means attention is paid to every detail. For example, flatware is heated or chilled for each course, depending upon the dish. It is chilled for a salad or cold dessert, and heated for soup and other hot foods. After the first few courses, a palate cleanser of sorbet is served in a small egg-shaped dish with twigs wrapped around the base. A warm, eucalyptus-scented hand towel also offers a bit of a breather between courses. The Five-Diamond mindset shows in the Riedel Sommelier hand-blown glassware as well as the sophisticated wine list.

Desert colors and shapes seen through the large windows are reflected in the table decor to show both the ancient and modern in understated elegance. The candle pot centerpiece is like the pottery, and the taller straight vase, bearing a single stem, represents the modern buildings.

The artwork in the dining room reflects the agricultural heritage, made even more specific in one-of-a-kind menus with watercolor paintings by local Pima artist Mike Medicine Horse Zillioux, each telling a different story of the culture. One menu cover tells a fishing story with symbols of the river and of corn. The circle of life is represented by a fish eye. Another shows men poking long sticks into the ground, followed by women dropping seeds into the holes.

Rather than listing courses on the menu as appetizers or entrees, the Kai menus are structured as "The Birth" (appetizers), "The Beginning" (first course), "The Journey" (second course) and "After Life" (dessert). In this book, however, the recipes are categorized in the more common cookbook format.

The bounty is endless. If you come to Kai, dine on the outdoor terrace or inside, order a Sundown at Komatke martini (named for the mountain you will see), and raise your glass to the people who were once here and those who are once again sharing the fruits of their heritage. Before you leave, your server will thank you ("Ma sap o") and say, "We'll see you again" ("Tho vah men yay").

Signature Cocktails

In addition to a world-class wine list to complement the distinctive flavors and textures of the cuisine at Kai, signature cocktails celebrate the agriculture of the desert, such as the especially flavorful citrus and the syrups made from desert plants that are combined with specialty liquors. These recipes make one generous drink.

⊙⊙⊙⊙⊙⊙⊙⊙⊙⊙⊙⊙⊙⊙⊙⊙⊙⊙⊙⊙⊙

Sundown at Komatke 27
Mesquite Bean Martini 28
The Great Fruit Martini 28
Mani Sahna 28
Waig 29
Aji Mojito 29
Chia Seed Lemonade 29

Sundown at Komatke

This colorful drink celebrates the nearby Komatke Mountain, the home of the wind to the people of the Gila River Indian Community.

Combine all ingredients except the macerated cranberry and shake over ice. Strain into a generous-sized martini glass and top with the cranberry.

2 ounces blood orange
   vodka
³/₄ ounce peach schnapps
³/₄ ounce Cointreau
Splash of piña colada mix
Splash of fresh orange juice
Macerated cranberry* for
   garnish

* Macerated cranberry refers to a cranberry that has been pre-soaked in a liqueur (such as Calvados or spiced rum) until soft.

Sundown at Komatke

Mesquite Bean Martini

1¼ ounces Ketel One vodka

1¼ ounces mesquite bean syrup (see Shopping Guide)

¾ ounce freshly squeezed lime juice

¾ ounce grapefruit juice

¼ ounce sweet vermouth

The versatile mesquite bean has long been a staple to the people of the Sonoran Desert. The thorny branches of the tree itself provide shelter for animals, and the resin from the bark is used to paint designs in Maricopa pottery. The bean provides sustenance, and its sweet syrup is used to flavor this martini.

Combine and shake ingredients over ice. Strain into a generous-sized martini glass.

The Great Fruit Martini

1 small grapefruit, peeled and cut into small pieces

¾ ounce freshly squeezed lime juice

¾ ounce Charbay grapefruit vodka

2 ounces Stolichnaya vanilla vodka

Splash of passion fruit puree

Dried grapefruit slice for garnish

The luscious citrus from Gila River Farms is freshly squeezed and muddled for this martini. It is garnished with a paper-thin slice of dried grapefruit.

Muddle the grapefruit pieces in a cocktail shaker by pressing them down with a wooden muddler or a spoon. Add the other ingredients and some ice cubes. Shake and strain into a generous-sized martini glass. Garnish with the grapefruit slice.

Mani Sahna

2 limes, peeled and cut into small pieces

3 ounces Van Gogh apple vodka

2 ounces apple schnapps

Apple juice

Green sugar and Martinelli sparkling cider for garnish

Mani Sahna is the Pima word for apple, and here three versions of the apple are combined for a drink that is at once sweet and tangy.

Muddle the lime pieces in a cocktail shaker by pressing them down with a wooden muddler or a spoon. Add the next 3 ingredients. Shake over ice. Rim the martini glass with the green sugar before pouring in the drink. Add a dash of the sparkling cider to finish with effervescence.

Waig

Waig is the Pima word for water, the source of prosperity for the people of the Gila River area, whose irrigation system thousands of years ago created an agricultural oasis in the desert.

Combine ingredients and shake over ice. Pour into generous martini glass. Garnish with a macerated cherry.

2 ounces Ultimat black
  cherry vodka
Splash of blue Curacao
4 ounces pineapple juice
Madeira-macerated cherry*
  for garnish

* Pitted fresh cherries can be soaked in Madeira for several hours until soft to make this garnish.

Aji Mojito

Aji is the name of the resort's spa, and it means sanctuary, a high place where the Maricopa people sent women and children in times of trouble. From this location they could survey what was going on. This drink is a toast to peace and sanctuary, and also to women and children.

Combine ingredients and shake lightly over ice. Serve in a tall beer glass. Garnish with mint leaves.

1¼ ounces freshly pressed
  lime juice
1¼ ounces simple syrup
1¼ ounces lychee puree*
1¼ ounces light rum
Mint leaves for garnish

*Canned lychee puree is available at specialty stores and online.

Chia Seed Lemonade

Chia seeds have a long history of nourishing the people of the desert. They were carried by native runners as a source of energy, and are often called "the running food." When the children at the Gila Crossing School first made this lemonade, they said, "It's like there are bugs in our juice." The seeds add fiber to your diet, and they also slow the absorption of sugars into the bloodstream. Thus, a refreshing drink with substance.

Mix all ingredients together and store in the refrigerator overnight. Pour over ice in a tall glass.

Makes a little more than a gallon

1 gallon apple juice
1 pint lemonade
2 ounces chia seeds (see
  Shopping Guide)

Breads

Fry bread and chemaith are the basic breads of the native people, although fry bread does not have a long history. It was created from the white flour and lard that the U.S. Army introduced the Indian people to along with canned goods. Nevertheless, making the best fry bread has taken on a competitive edge, with many insisting, "My grandma made it better than yours." These large, puffy circles of crisp-edged bread are a bit like the tandoori oven–baked nan of the Indian subcontinent. Fry bread has also been compared with tortillas and pita bread. It is often eaten as a snack with sugar or honey. When filled with meat, vegetables, spices, and cheese, it becomes the "Indian Taco" sold at fairs and festivals throughout the Southwest.

Blue cornmeal is another favorite in native cooking, and at Kai it is given a new sophistication as a base for scones.

⊙⊙⊙⊙⊙⊙⊙⊙⊙⊙⊙⊙⊙⊙⊙⊙⊙⊙⊙⊙

Third-Generation Fry Bread

Traditionally made with lard and deep-fried like a doughnut, fry bread varies from chewy and fluffy in texture to crunchy and crisp. At Kai it is soft and fluffy with a slight crunch on the outside, and a consistency similar to that of a popover. The restaurant serves fry bread as a base for Butter-Basted Lobster (page 63) and also with a dessert of Ibarra Chocolate with Kahlúa Ice Cream and Ancho Caramel Sauce (page 95). The name comes from one of the restaurant's first cooks, Jesse Zillioux, a young man from the native community who developed it from what he learned from his mother and grandmother.

4 cups Bluebird or all-purpose flour
2 tablespoons baking powder
1 teaspoon salt
3 tablespoons lard
1 cup warm mineral water
1/2 cup whole milk
4 cups oil for frying, such as canola

1. Combine flour, baking powder, and salt in a large bowl. Cut in the lard using a fork or two knives until you have a crumbly consistency. Add water and milk and mix until dough forms a ball. Knead by hand in the bowl no more than 10 times, forming a smooth ball that is not sticky. Cover the dough with a damp cloth and allow it to rest at room temperature for 30 minutes.

2. Heat oil in a deep-fryer, Dutch oven, or large deep skillet to 350 degrees.

3. Pull a small knob from the dough and, on a floured surface, form it into a round shape about 5 or 6 inches in diameter and of the desired thickness. The thinner it is, the crispier it will be. (Some use a rolling pin to flatten out the dough, but the traditional way is to flatten it by hand.)

4. Place the dough gently into the hot oil and, using tongs, cook on both sides until golden brown, about 2 minutes per side. Drain on a plate lined with paper towels. Repeat the process until all the dough has been used.

Makes 16 to 18 pieces

Chef Strong Notes: It's best to eat fry bread right away, or it will lose its delicate flavor and consistency. However, you can make the dough ahead of time and store it in the refrigerator overnight.

Chemaith Bread

4 cups Bluebird or all-
purpose flour

1 tablespoon salt

2 tablespoons baking
powder

2 tablespoons vegetable
shortening

2 cups warm mineral or
filtered water

Chemaith might be described as a cross between a tortilla and a crêpe. A traditional bread made by the Pima and Maricopa people, the recipe for chemaith was passed along from one generation to the next, but never written down. Chefs at Kai worked with Gila River Indian Community elders until they got it just right.

For best flavor, chemaith should be made with Bluebird flour, but you can use all-purpose flour if necessary. Chemaith is similar to pita bread but not as soft, and is good for breaking up and serving with dips at parties. At Kai, chemaith is made a bit thicker than is traditional so that other ingredients can be added into the dough, such as chile puree, olives, or even dried fruit. Here is the basic recipe with some variations.

1. Preheat the oven to 350 degrees.

2. Sift the dry ingredients together in a large bowl. Add the shortening and warm water and work with your hands until you get a workable dough.

3. For each chemaith, pull a ball from the dough and flatten it with your hands until it is about 3 inches in diameter and about ¼ inch thick.

4. Cook on a hot grill or cast-iron skillet until the bread puffs slightly and is brown. Once all the pieces are cooked on the grill, arrange them on a sheet pan and finish in the oven for about 5 minutes.

Makes about 30 three-inch pieces

Chef Strong Notes: You can also make crispy crackers from this dough by rolling it out very thin before cooking.

To Serve

At Kai, chemaith is served on a plate with an overlapping smaller dish of the local olive oil to which a few seeds and nuts have been added.

CHEMAITH BREAD VARIATIONS

Olive Chemaith

Omit the salt from the basic recipe and add about ¾ cup Gila River (or similar) olive tapenade to the dough after the other ingredients have been combined.

Chile Chemaith

Add 4 to 5 tablespoons Piquillo Pepper chile puree (see page 108) to the basic dough after the other ingredients have been combined.

Dried Fruit Chemaith

Use your favorite dried fruit such as chopped apples, pears, apricots, raisins, or even some berries.

Chop the dried fruit to a small dice in a food processor. Combine the chopped fruit, wine, honey, and cinnamon stick in a saucepan with water to cover. Bring to a boil and lower heat. Simmer on low to medium heat until the fruit is soft. Drain, cool, and add to the basic chemaith dough.

1½ cups dried fruit, chopped
1 cup port wine
1 cup honey
1 cinnamon stick
Water to cover

Cornbread Pudding

The charred chiles and the cheese give this pudding a robust taste and tex-ture that complements the rack of lamb at Kai, but it will complement other dishes as well. While it is a bit complex, you can break this recipe into manageable steps and do some of it ahead of time. Be sure you don't add the eggs until just before the pudding goes into the oven, or the bread will get too soft.

3 ancho chiles

3 cups whole milk

3 Anaheim chiles

Oil for the grill

Salt and pepper to taste

4 to 6 tablespoons canola oil

¼ cup minced garlic

1 yellow onion, medium-diced

1½ pounds white and brown clamshell mushrooms (see Chef's Note)

Small bunch fresh thyme

1 head of garlic, cut in half

3½ cups cheddar cheese, shredded

½ sheet pan recipe for Cornbread (see page 35), cut into 1-inch squares

1 tablespoon butter (approximate)

12 eggs

1. Put the anchos in a bowl with the milk to soak. Later, before adding them to the pudding mixture, strain the milk out, dice the anchos, and set aside. Char the Anaheim chiles on an oiled grill with some salt and pepper. Put them in a bowl covered with plastic wrap until cool. Then peel, seed, and dice the chiles.

2. Sauté the minced garlic and yellow onions in 1 tablespoon of canola oil until translucent. Put them into a large bowl and set aside.

3. Clean the mushrooms, remove and discard stems, and slice the caps. Heat 2 or 3 tablespoons of oil in a pan and sauté the mushrooms with thyme, the garlic head halves, salt, and pepper. Cook over medium heat until tender, about 5 or 6 minutes. Discard the thyme and garlic, and add the mushrooms to the reserved bowl with the minced garlic and yellow onions. Add the shredded cheddar and diced chile peppers to the bowl.

4. Preheat the oven to 375 degrees. Toss the cornbread squares in a bowl with 2 tablespoons oil, salt, and pepper. Spread the squares on a sheet pan and bake for 10 to 12 minutes, rotating once during this time so the squares toast evenly. Allow them to cool before combining with the mushrooms, cheese, chile peppers, minced garlic, and onions.

5. Line a 9 x 11-inch baking pan with a piece of parchment paper and butter the paper thoroughly.

6. Break the eggs into a separate bowl and whisk until blended. Reserve about ¼ cup and set aside.

7. Add the beaten eggs to the bowl with the bread, mushrooms, cheese, chile peppers, minced garlic, and onions. Gently mix all the ingredients together so as not to break up the bread cubes, but be sure they are coated well with the liquid mix. Pour the mixture into the pan, brush the reserved egg over the top, cover with foil, and bake at 375 degrees for 40 to 60 minutes. Rotate the pan in 15 minutes and then again in another 15 minutes. After the second rotation, remove the foil and bake for an additional 10 minutes or until the center of the pudding is firm.

To Serve

When the pudding has thoroughly cooled, overturn the pan onto a flat surface. Use a ring mold to cut individual portions. If serving with lamb or other meat, place one portion in the center of a large plate and lean the meat against it.

Serves 8

Chef O'Dowd Notes:
Clamshell mushrooms are Asian in origin and, whether brown or white, have a nutty flavor and crisp texture. They grow in clusters with long stems and small caps. They are available from many gourmet markets or online. A similar type of mushroom, pioppino, may be substituted.

Kai Cornbread

At Kai, this cornbread is made especially for Cornbread Pudding, which is served with the Pecan-Crusted Roasted Colorado Rack of Lamb on page 75. The flat cornbread is baked on a sheet pan and cut into squares and toasted before it goes into the pudding.

1. Preheat the oven to 350 degrees. Grease a sheet pan with 1-inch or higher sidewalls.
2. In a large bowl, blend the dry ingredients. In another bowl, mix together the eggs and milk. Add the dry ingredients to the liquid and mix until smooth. Pour the batter onto the pan and bake for about 12 minutes.

Makes 1 average sheet pan

Butter to grease the pan
4 cups Bluebird (see Shopping Guide) or all-purpose flour
4 cups cornmeal
4 teaspoons sea salt
3 tablespoons baking powder
1 cup sugar
8 eggs, lightly beaten
4 cups milk

1½ cups all-purpose flour

1¼ cups sugar

1 teaspoon baking powder

½ teaspoon salt

4 ounces (1 stick) cold
butter

1 cup chopped almonds

4 eggs, lightly beaten

2 teaspoons vanilla extract

2 teaspoons almond extract

2 teaspoons lemon extract

2 teaspoons orange extract

1 cup huitlacoche puree
(see Chef's Note)

Water

½ cup large-crystal sugar*
for garnish

Oil or butter to grease the
sheet pan

* Large-crystal sugars are widely
available in bakery sections of
most supermarkets and gourmet
stores.

Huitlacoche Biscotti

*Most of us know biscotti as an Italian delicacy that has become popular
in American coffee shops in recent years. Here, biscotti are given a new
twist with* huitlacoche *and served at Kai to complement Chilled Sixty-Day
Sweet Corn Soup (page 60) or Fire-Roasted Corn Crème Brûlée (page 96).
These biscotti are ideal for serving at a party with a variety of accompany-
ing dips, such as the Black Bean Hummus on page 38. They are simple to
prepare, but make them a couple of days ahead, because you need to let them
set in various stages and bake them twice (biscotti means "twice baked" in
Italian). They will keep well in a cool, dry place. This recipe will make two
"logs" which you can store and slice when ready to bake.*

1. Preheat the oven to 350 degrees. Mix the flour, sugar, baking powder, and salt in a large bowl. Cut in the cold butter with a fork or two
knives until you have a crumbly consistency. Add the almonds, eggs,
extracts, and huitlacoche puree and mix it into a dough. Divide the
dough and form it into two log shapes; brush with water, and sprinkle
with sugar crystals. Bake on a greased sheet pan for 15 minutes. Turn
the logs over and cook for another 15 minutes.

2. Allow the logs to cool and then wrap in tin foil or plastic wrap. Store
the logs overnight in the refrigerator so they will hold their form well
when you slice them before baking. The next day, slice the logs verti-
cally about ¼ inch thick and rebake the slices on a greased sheet pan
at 300 degrees until crisp. You should have about 24 slices from each
log.

3. Allow the baked slices to cool for a few hours, or even better, overnight. Stored in a cool, dry place, the biscotti will keep for months.

Makes 4 or 5 dozen

◎◎

Chef Strong Notes: Huitlacoche, also spelled as cuitlacoche, is a fungus
known as corn smut that was a great favorite of the ancient Aztecs and
is considered a delicacy in Mexico, with flavor that has been described
as inky and mushroomy. It is widely available canned in Mexican and
gourmet markets.

◎◎

Appetizers

These are some of "The Beginning" dishes served at Kai. At home you may want to use them not only as appetizers or small plates, but even as a light lunch. The Lion's Paw Baja Scallops recipe can be increased to become a main course.

⊙⊙⊙⊙⊙⊙⊙⊙⊙⊙⊙⊙⊙⊙⊙⊙⊙⊙⊙⊙⊙⊙⊙

Black Bean Hummus 38

Three Sisters Composition: Sweet Corn Panna Cotta, Pickled Local Squash,
and Venison Carpaccio 39

Tres Pescados Ceviche from the Sea of Cortez 42

Dried Mango and Sandalwood-Dusted Lion's Paw Baja Scallops
with Poached Salsify and Ojo de Cabra Mud 44

Hudson Valley Foie Gras and Pumpkin Brûlée 46

Buffalo Tartare with Prairie Quail Egg and Kai Sweet and Sour Sauce 49

Black Bean Hummus

This dish is an adaptation of a well-known Middle Eastern staple. While it is not on the Kai menu, it is a popular dish served often at the resort for parties and banquets. It is an ideal mate for Chemaith bread, which can be used as a scoop for the dip.

In a blender, puree all the ingredients, adding the oil at the end to finish. Serve the hummus with Chemaith (page 32).

Makes about 2 cups

1/2 cup chopped cipollini onions (see Chef's Note)

1 cup cooked garbanzo beans, drained

1 cup cooked black beans, drained

1/2 head garlic, peeled

1/2 tablespoon chipotle adobe pepper

1/2 tablespoon ground cumin

2 tablespoons minced fresh basil leaves

2 tablespoons minced fresh cilantro leaves

3 lemons, juiced

2 limes, juiced

Salt and pepper to taste

1/4 cup olive oil (approximate)

⊚⊚

Chef O'Dowd Notes: I like cipollini onions because they have more residual sugars than the garden-variety white or yellow onions. Because they are harvested in the fall, you may not be able to get them all year. In that case, substitute shallots.

⊚⊚

Three Sisters Composition: Sweet Corn Panna Cotta, Pickled Local Squash, and Venison Carpaccio

The "three sisters"—corn, beans, and squash—are the basis for much of Native American cuisine, and here the combination gets a new twist. The Corn Panna Cotta complements the Pickled Local Squash (page 89), and the beans are the base for the mole powder in the Venison Carpaccio. Make the panna cotta and pickled squash in advance and put them together with the venison just before serving.

Sweet Corn Panna Cotta

6 sheets gelatin (see Chef's
   Note)

5 ears corn, roasted

1 cup buttermilk

3 cups heavy cream

1 to 1½ teaspoons honey,
   or to taste

Salt to taste

Oil to lubricate mold

⊙⊙⊙⊙⊙⊙⊙⊙⊙⊙⊙⊙⊙⊙

Chef O'Dowd Notes:
Sheet gelatin has always
been more popular in
Europe than in this
country, possibly because
it needs to soak longer
than the powdered
type, but it is gaining
popularity here. It creates
far better results than
the powdered variety,
especially for a delicate
panna cotta. Four sheets
are the equivalent of one
package of powdered
gelatin.

⊙⊙⊙⊙⊙⊙⊙⊙⊙⊙⊙⊙⊙⊙

Panna cotta, Italian for "cooked cream," is a light, silky, eggless custard that can be the base for savory as well as sweet dishes. It can be tricky to get just the right consistency, but once you've mastered it, you can use panna cotta to create many unforgettable dishes. Combined with roasted corn flavor, it is a perfect complement to meat dishes, as well as being part of a Three Sisters Composition.

1. Place the gelatin sheets in a bowl of cold water to make them "bloom" or soften. Set aside for 5 to 10 minutes.

2. Roast the corn in the husks over an outdoor grill, or wrapped in foil in a 350-degree oven for about 15 minutes. Let the corn cool before removing the husks. Cut the corn kernels from the cobs and put them in a large pot with the buttermilk and cream. Cut up the cobs and add them to the pot. Bring to a boil and immediately lower the heat to simmer for about an hour to bring out as much of the corn flavor as possible.

3. Discard the cobs and puree the mixture with a stick blender right in the pot. Add honey to taste. The amount will depend upon the sweetness of the corn, but on average about 1 to 1½ teaspoons should suffice. Strain the mixture through a fine sieve and add salt to taste.

4. Remove the gelatin sheets from the cold water and remove excess water from the sheets with a towel. If necessary, reheat the corn mixture so it is hot. Add the bloomed gelatin and whisk to dissolve thoroughly. Pour the mixture into a greased mold about half full and refrigerate overnight. At Kai individual triangular molds are used, but at home you can put it all in one mold, such as a soufflé dish, and then cut the panna cotta into desired shapes when you serve it.

To Serve

Put a warm towel under the mold for a minute or two to loosen the panna cotta, then gently overturn the mold onto a large flat plate. Slice or use a ring mold to cut the panna cotta into individual portions.

Venison Carpaccio

Season the venison with salt and pepper and generously rub it with the Mole Dust. In a hot sauté pan with a little oil, sear the tenderloin on all sides. Then remove it from the pan and put it in the freezer for at least an hour.

To Serve

Slice the frozen venison paper-thin and place it on the bottom of each serving dish. Place a scoop of the panna cotta on top of the venison and sprinkle some of the squash pickles around the plate. Or place each component separately on a long dish and garnish with micro greens.

A crisp Pinot Grigio would suit this dish and honor the Italian influence.

Serves 6

1 tenderloin of venison
Salt and pepper to taste
1/4 cup Mole Dust (see page 110)
Oil for frying
Corn Panna Cotta
Pickled Local Squash (page 89)

Tres Pescados Ceviche from the Sea of Cortez

Ceviche (also spelled seviche or cebeche) originated in Peru and was standard fare throughout South and Central America before it became popular all over the world. The word means to saturate the fish, which is a way of cooking it in citrus juice. You can use any fish as long as it is absolutely fresh. Always ask for sushi quality when you buy it. Smell the fish to be sure it is fresh. White fish that keeps its shape and texture such as snapper, sea bass, halibut, scallops and shark are best. Soft fish like sole can become mushy. At Kai the three fishes used for this flavorful dish are yellowtail tuna, corvina, and shark. Corvina has a firm white flesh, high fat content, and a mildly sweet flavor. Mako and thresher shark are among the most widely used for ceviches. For ceviche, you can dice or slice the fish. If sliced, it must be paper-thin, less than ¼ inch if possible. You need a very sharp knife. For this recipe, the tuna is chopped and the other fish is sliced, which adds interesting and different textures to the dish. The tuna preparation is the most involved, so make it first; the other two ceviches can be prepared just before serving.

Yellowtail Ceviche

1. Combine the juice of 2 oranges and 2 limes with the lavender vinegar. Add the diced yellowtail and marinate for about 10 minutes. Set aside.

2. In a mixing bowl, combine the mango, the remaining orange and lime juice, the papaya, yellow tomato, and herbs. Remove the yellowtail from the original marinade and add it to the bowl with the Chihuacle Negro Puree, salt, and pepper.

4 oranges, juiced

3 limes, juiced

¼ cup Basic Lavender Vinegar (see page 102)

1½ pounds yellowtail tuna fillet, diced medium

1 mango, diced small

1 papaya, diced small

1 yellow tomato, diced small

½ teaspoon finely chopped fresh basil

½ teaspoon finely chopped mint

½ teaspoon finely chopped cilantro

2 teaspoons Chihuacle Negro Puree (see page 108)

Salt and pepper to taste

Shark Ceviche

Prepare a serving-size portion of the shark, about the size of a business card. This would be a 2- to 3-ounce piece, about 4 inches long, and not more than ¼ inch thick (the thinner the slice, the better). Marinate the shark in the vinegar and oil mixture for about 10 minutes.

1½ pounds shark fillet, sliced thin into 6 portions
Few splashes of extra-virgin olive oil
½ cup Banana Vinegar (see Chef's Note)

⊙⊙⊙

Chef O'Dowd Notes: Banana vinegar is a traditional ingredient in Caribbean cooking. We make it ourselves at Kai and add vanilla bean to make the flavor more complex. However, it is difficult to make at home so look for ready-made banana vinegar in ethnic stores and at Whole Foods Markets.

⊙⊙⊙

Corvina Ceviche

Cut the corvina into thin slices about the size of a business card (as described for the shark, above). Marinate the corvina slices in the citrus juice.

1½ pounds corvina fillet, cut into 6 paper-thin slices
2 oranges, juiced
2 limes, juiced
Micro cilantro and mint (see Chef's Note)

To Serve

Use a rectangular plate with enough room for the three ceviches to show up nicely. Place a mound of the Yellowtail Ceviche in the center of the plate, and position the slices of Corvina and Shark Ceviches on either side. Garnish with micro cilantro and mint.

Serves 6

⊙⊙⊙⊙⊙⊙⊙⊙⊙⊙⊙⊙⊙⊙

Chef Strong Notes: At Kai we have a regular supply of micro greens and herbs to use as garnish. These baby plants are sometimes available in gourmet stores. If you cannot get fresh micro greens or herbs, use the smallest leaf or sprig from the fully grown variety of plant.

⊙⊙⊙⊙⊙⊙⊙⊙⊙⊙⊙⊙⊙⊙

Dried Mango and Sandalwood-Dusted Lion's Paw Baja Scallops with Poached Salsify and Ojo de Cabra Mud

Lion's paw scallops are taller and thinner than diver's scallops, with a sweeter flavor. Combined with the dried mango, sandalwood dust, and other East Indian and Caribbean spices, this makes a very aromatic dish. As an appetizer, two scallops per dish are needed, but you can also increase this to a main course using five scallops per person. You will have more than enough of the Dried Mango and Sandalwood Dust (see page 110), so store the rest in a jar for use next time or on any white fish, or even with a pork dish. You can also make the "mud" and salsify ahead of time.

Ojo de Cabra Mud

Ojo de Cabra means "eye of the goat." These light brown beans keep their color when made into a thick puree, which has a sweet flavor.

1 pound of Ojo de Cabra beans, soaked overnight (see Glossary and Shopping Guide)
Water for soaking and boiling beans
1 head of garlic, cut in half
1 or more tablespoons salt for boiling water
1 bunch fresh thyme
Salt to taste

1. Drain the beans from the soaking water and place in a saucepan. Cover with fresh water and add garlic and thyme. Season the water with plenty of salt as you would for boiling pasta. Cook the beans until tender, about 45 minutes to 1 hour.

2. Strain the beans and puree them in a blender, adding water if necessary for a mud-like consistency. Add salt to taste and set aside.

Poached Salsify

Salsify is a root vegetable that looks a bit like a parsnip, only it's bigger and has darker skin. It is also called the oyster plant because of its flavor. Select salsify that is heavy for its size. It will keep for about a week in the fridge wrapped in plastic. You can find it at Spanish, Greek, and Italian markets.

1 large salsify root
1 cup heavy cream
1 cup whole milk
1 head of garlic, cut in half
1 bunch fresh thyme
1 lemon, sliced in half

1. Peel the salsify and cut it into 2-inch logs. Using a mandolin, peel off a few thin shavings from the already peeled root and set them aside to fry for garnish (see below). Then make thin slices from the logs. Slice lengthwise so you have planks about ⅛ inch thick.

2. In a saucepan, bring the cream, milk, garlic, thyme, and lemon to a simmer. Place the salsify planks into the simmering mixture and cook them until tender, about 5 or 6 minutes. Cool the planks in the poaching liquid and strain before using.

Lion's Paw Scallops

1. Preheat the oven to 350 degrees.

2. In a small bowl, coat the scallops by rolling each one around in the Dried Mango and Sandalwood Dust.

3. In a hot oiled sauté pan, sear each scallop at top and bottom, about 2 minutes per side. Finish the scallops in the oven until cooked through, about 5 to 6 minutes.

4. Use the same sauté pan to fry the salsify peelings for a garnish. When crisp, drain and reserve the salsify curls on a paper towel.

5. Meanwhile, heat the Ojo de Cabra Mud in a small saucepan.

6. In another small saucepan, heat the salsify planks in the reserved poaching liquid.

To Serve

Spoon a small amount of the warm Ojo de Cabra Mud in the middle of each wide dinner bowl. Place two salsify planks side by side on top of the mud. Place two cooked scallops on top of the salsify planks in each bowl and garnish with mâche greens. Drizzle fennel oil over the dish and dust a bit of fennel powder around the bowl. Top the dish with crisped salsify peels and serve.

Serves 4

Dried Mango and
  Sandalwood Dust (page
  110)
8 lion's paw scallops
2 to 3 tablespoons
  canola oil
8 planks Poached Salsify
Ojo de Cabra Mud
Salsify curls
1 cup mâche greens,
  washed and dried
Fennel oil (see page 103)
Fennel powder (see Chef's
  Note)

Chef Strong Notes:
Fennel pollen powder is made from the flowers of the plant. This fragrant powder adds the finishing touch to an already aromatic dish. You can find dried fennel flowers in specialty stores. At home, simply toast them in a dry sauté pan for a few minutes and grind them to powder in a coffee grinder. Mix them with a little oil and make a drizzle to use as garnish.

Hudson Valley Foie Gras and Pumpkin Brûlée

The combination of pumpkin and foie gras is a favorite at Kai. To the Native Americans, pumpkin is an "isoquotm squash," and therefore one of the "three sisters" trinity. They used all of the pumpkin. The skin was flattened and dried and woven into mats. The toasted seeds were a favorite snack as well as a good "medicine" for curing snakebite and other ills.

At Kai we serve this with Hatch chiles, lavender tuilles, and macerated cranberries. You can prepare most components of this recipe in advance and assemble it just before serving. You will need a brûlée torch for this one.

1 lobe of grade A foie gras

1 cup port wine

½ bunch fresh thyme

Salt and pepper to taste

1 cup sugar

1 Guajillo chile (see Glossary and Shopping Guide)

1 Moro Rojo chile (see Glossary and Shopping Guide)

½ tablespoon Santa Cruz chili powder (mild)

½ tablespoon chili powder

½ tablespoon Hatch chili powder (mild)

1 cup water

½ cup peeled, seeded, and diced fresh pumpkin

Lavender Tuilles (see page 115)

Macerated cranberries (see page 27)

1. Bring the lobe of foie gras to room temperature. Wearing kitchen gloves, break the lobe apart with your fingers. Pull out the blood vessels and then put the lobe into a bowl with the port wine and thyme. Season with salt and pepper and set aside in the refrigerator.

2. In a saucepan combine the sugar, chiles, and chili powders with the water and bring to a boil. Lower the heat and simmer for about 20 minutes to create a chili-infused simple syrup. Strain this through a fine sieve lined with a coffee filter into another pot and bring the water back to a boil. Pour this hot syrup over the diced pumpkin and let it sit for about 20 minutes until the pumpkin is tender.

3. Remove the foie gras from the port wine and thyme marinade and put it into the bowl of a mixer. Using the paddle attachment, whip up the foie gras. The paddle will catch more veins, so remove the whipped foie gras into another bowl and mix in the blanched pumpkin, being careful not to break up the pumpkin. Refrigerate until set, about 1 hour.

To Serve

Spoon about 2 tablespoons of the pumpkin foie gras mixture into each small serving bowl or ramekin. Lay some plastic wrap on top and press down. Just before serving, remove the plastic wrap, and finish with the brûlée torch at the table (with obvious caution). Put a tuille on one side of each plate and a spoonful of macerated cranberries on the other, and serve. At Kai we give this dish a little added drama by igniting a marshmallow atop the dish.

Serves 6 or 8

Buffalo Tartare with Prairie Quail Egg and Kai Sweet and Sour Sauce

Buffalo meat is leaner and sweeter than beef and has less cholesterol. However, you can use this same recipe with Kobe beef if you like. The cornichons and fried caper berries add some sweetness and tang to the dish.

1. Wrap the garlic head in tin foil and roast it in a 350-degree oven. When soft, remove four cloves from the head, peel and mash them, and set aside.

2. Make a *brunoise* of the shallots and *nopalitas,* by sautéing them slowly in the butter over a medium heat until tender.

3. Combine the garlic, brunoise, diced buffalo tenderloin, capers, anchovies, and mustard in a bowl and add salt and pepper to taste.

4. Sauté the quail eggs in a nonstick pan until firm.

To Serve

For each serving, place a portion of the buffalo mixture into a ring mold, tuna can size, and center it on the plate. Unmold, top with a quail egg and sprinkle with fried caper berries and cornichons, and drizzle some Kai Sweet and Sour Sauce around the plate. (At Kai the buffalo tartare is served in cones made with cornmeal.)

Pair this with a light red wine such as Bordeaux from Margaus or Nebbiolo from Italy. An earthy Burgundy would also complement the dish.

Serves 4

8 teaspoons finely diced shallots

4 teaspoons finely diced nopalitas (pickled cactus pads)

2 tablespoons salt-free butter

1 garlic head

12 ounces center-cut buffalo tenderloin, diced small

4 teaspoons crushed capers

2 anchovy fillets, cut fine

2 teaspoons grain mustard

Salt and pepper to taste

4 quail eggs

8 caper berries, fried crisp

8 cornichons

2 teaspoons Kai Sweet and Sour Sauce (page 106)

From The Fields:
Salads And Soups

The early Pima and Maricopa probably did not make salads as we know them today, but they gathered plenty of wild greens and other plants to serve with their meals. *Verdolagas,* for example, are known throughout the Southwest, but this sweet, milk herb is known as purslane in the rest of the world. The salad green that today's chefs and foodies call mâche also grows throughout the region, sometimes wild in the cornfields. Tiny baby greens of tumbleweed and dandelion, even tender yucca blossoms, were used by the native people, and these make wonderful salad ingredients. The immature pods of prickly pear cactus, which taste a bit like zucchini or green beans, are popularly known as nopales and widely used in salads.

At Kai the tender salad greens and herbs come from the Gila Crossing School children's farm, and the corn and squash used for soups are from the Tohono O'odham people in the far south of Arizona. Soups of the native people tend to be robust, and there is an overlap between soup and stew.

Recipes in this section can be served as beginnings to a meal, but are also good as light lunches.

⊙⊙⊙⊙⊙⊙⊙⊙⊙⊙⊙⊙⊙⊙⊙⊙⊙⊙⊙⊙⊙⊙⊙

Salad of Baby Lettuces with Foie Gras Date Cake and Goat Cheese

Unless you live near the Gila River, you won't be able to use the baby greens that are hand-picked by the children of the Gila Crossing School (see Chapter 2), but for this salad choose the freshest baby greens you can find such as Lollo Rossa, red leaf, or green leaf lettuce. These tender greens pair wonderfully with the tangy and smoky blood orange vinaigrette. Garnish the salad with the foie gras date cake, which you can make ahead, and goat cheese. This salad is served with Blood Orange Vinaigrette, but it is also delicious with the Saguaro-Lavender Vinaigrette on page 104.

1 lobe grade A foie gras, cleaned (see page 46)
2 cups vintage port wine
30 Turkish dates, pitted
2 local oranges, zested
Sea salt and pepper to taste

3 cups (approximate) baby greens such as red and green oak, Lolla Rossa, and red leaf romaine
2 tablespoons fresh chives, chopped
Blood Orange Vinaigrette (see page 103)
Sea salt and fresh black pepper
6 slices Humboldt Fog goat cheese (see Chef's Note)
6 slices Foie Gras Date Cake

Foie Gras Date Cake

Bring the lobe of cleaned foie gras to room temperature. In a bowl, pour the Port over the dates and marinate for 2 hours. Remove the dates from the liquor and puree them in a food processor with the foie gras and orange zest. Season with sea salt and ground pepper. Store in the refrigerator until ready to use.

Salad of Baby Greens

1. Gently rinse the greens in cool water and let them air-dry or pat them with a clean towel.
2. Just before serving, gently toss the greens and chives in a bowl with some of the Blood Orange Vinaigrette. Season with salt and pepper.

To Serve

Stack some greens in layers in the center of each round dinner-size plate. On one side place a slice (or some crumbles) of the goat cheese and on the other side, a slice of the Foie Gras Date Cake. Drizzle some of the vinaigrette around the edge of the plate.

Serves 6

Chef O'Dowd Notes: Humboldt Fog goat cheese is named for the legendary fog that rolls into the San Francisco area from Humboldt Bay. It's a mold–ripened cheese with a layer of edible ash in the middle. It is light and slightly lemony with a hint of goat.

Wood-Grilled Butternut Squash Puree with Wild Boar Bacon, Rio Zape Beans, and Pima Cotton Candy

At Kai this soup—or puree, as it is called—is poured over a small mound of the bean and bacon mixture and the puff of cotton candy, which represents the cotton harvest of the Pima tribe. The flavor key here is the wood-grilled squash. The fun part is watching the cotton candy dissolve in the warm soup. The cotton candy is made at Kai and is optional here unless you have access to a cotton candy–making machine or a store that carries bagged cotton candy. This is a rather complex recipe, but well worth the effort. To simplify things, make the bacon and bean mixture ahead of time. The TOCA butternut squash used at Kai is grown by the Tohono O'odham people in southern Arizona from heirloom seeds described in Chapter 2.

Beans and Bacon

1. Simmer the pre-soaked beans in salted mineral water with the fresh thyme and the halved garlic head until tender, about 2 hours. Strain the beans, remove the garlic and thyme twigs, and then put half of the beans into a blender. Add enough water to make a thick puree. Pour the puree into a bowl, fold in the whole beans and piquillo peppers, and set aside.

2. Sauté the bacon over medium heat until cooked through and crisp. Drain on paper towels and set aside. Just before serving, crumble the bacon and mix the bits into the bean puree.

1 pound Rio Zape beans (see Glossary), soaked overnight

Mineral water, enough to cover beans plus 1 inch

1 tablespoon salt (approximate)

1 bunch fresh thyme

1 head garlic, cut in half

$^1/_2$ cup grilled and diced piquillo peppers (see Glossary)

1 cup diced wild boar bacon (see Shopping Guide)

Wood-Grilled Butternut Squash Puree

1. Place wet mesquite chips on a hot gas grill and allow to cook until smoke begins to emerge from the chips. Place the squash slices on the grill and cook a few minutes on each side to get grill marks and a smoky flavor. Set aside.

2. In a large pot sauté the onion, celery, carrots, garlic cloves, and shallots in oil. Add both rojo chiles to the pot along with the grilled squash. Add the chicken stock and simmer until the squash is cooked through, about 10 minutes. Put into a blender and puree, or use a stick blender in the pot. Strain the mixture through a fine sieve back into the pot and add the heavy cream, lime juice, salt and pepper to taste. Pour into a serving pitcher.

To Serve

Put a small mound (about ½ cup) of the bean puree into the bottom of each wide soup bowl. Top each mound with a puff of cotton candy if you have it. Then generously sprinkle the ground aji amarillo chili spice on top. After the plate is served to your guest, pour the warm soup into the bowl. (For an elegant touch, pour each serving from a small ceramic pitcher.)

A sweet Riesling pairs well with this dish and balances the smoki-ness of the squash.

Serves 8

4 cups mesquite chips, soaked in water

5 small to medium butternut squashes, peeled and cut into 1-inch slices

1 yellow onion, sliced

3 stalks celery, roughly chopped

3 carrots, peeled and roughly chopped

14 cloves garlic, peeled

6 shallots, sliced

2 to 3 tablespoons canola oil

2 Mojo Rojo chiles (see Glossary), one seeded and one whole

3½ quarts chicken stock

2 pints heavy cream

1 lime, juiced

Salt and pepper to taste

¼ cup chiffonade of opal basil

1 tablespoon aji amarillo chili powder (see Glossary)

Cotton candy if available

Confit of Heirloom Tomatoes and Sun Roots with High Country Mushroom Espresso

Confit is an ancient method of preserving meat such as goose and duck by salting it and slowly cooking it in its own fat. It is then stored in a crock and covered with the fat so it is sealed and preserved in the refrigerator for as long as six months. While it is an excellent way to preserve food, it also brings out the intense flavors. Here, the combination of heirloom tomatoes and Jerusalem artichokes (also known as sun roots) "confit" in local olive oil makes an exceptional dish. You will need some individual ring molds to layer it on the plate with boar bacon in the middle and a quail egg on top. It is served with a cup of "espresso" made of dried mushrooms ground to a powder and white miso soup. It's an ideal brunch dish.

Confit of Tomatoes and Sun Roots

1. Preheat the oven to 300 degrees.

2. Heat the oil in a deep sauté pan or wide saucepan. Score the tomatoes and dip them into the hot oil to make it easier to remove the skin. When cool, seed and quarter the tomatoes. Put them into a roasting pan with the garlic, thyme, salt, and peppercorns. Roast for about 20 to 25 minutes. Be careful not to overcook them, or you will have mushy tomatoes. Let the tomatoes cool, then dice them and set aside.

3. Put the peeled and diced sun roots into the same pan of oil used to peel the tomatoes. Simmer over very low heat to "confit" the sun roots, about 20 minutes or until tender. Strain the oil from the sun roots and combine them with the tomatoes in a bowl. Season with salt and pepper.

4. Turn the oven up to 350 degrees and put the bacon slices on a sheet pan and roast until crisp, about 20 minutes. Drain on a paper towel.

5. Crack the quail eggs onto a non-stick sauté pan and cook them over-easy.

To Serve

Use two ring molds for each serving, one smaller than the other. Fill each with the confit mixture. In the middle of each large dinner bowl, unmold the larger mold and top it with 1 piece of the bacon. Unmold the smaller mold on top of the bacon and top that with 1 quail egg. Finish with a sprinkle of black sea salt on the yolk and a few thoughtfully placed sprigs of micro celery. Serve each with a demitasse cup of Mushroom Miso Espresso Soup.

Olive oil to cover, 1 to 2 cups (approximate)

3 large ripe heirloom tomatoes

1 head garlic, cut in half

Fresh thyme

½ teaspoon salt

1 tablespoon peppercorns

1 cup peeled, diced small Jerusalem artichokes (sun roots)

4 slices wild boar bacon or thick-cut regular bacon

4 quail eggs

Black Hawaiian sea salt for garnish

Micro celery for garnish (see Chef's Note)

1 cup dried mushrooms,
  such as porcini or
  chanterelle
2 quarts mineral water
2 cups white miso paste
¼ cup chiffonade of Swiss
  chard leaves
¼ cup thinly bias-sliced
  green onion
¼ cup chopped chives

Mushroom Miso Espresso Soup

1. Using a coffee grinder, make a fine powder of the dried mushrooms. Set aside.

2. Bring the mineral water to a boil in a saucepan and whisk in the miso paste. Set aside and keep warm.

To Serve

Put 1 teaspoon mushroom powder into each espresso cup along with equal parts of the chiffonade of Swiss chard, green onion, and chives. At table, pour the miso soup into the espresso cup and stir.

Serves 4

Chef O'Dowd Notes: Micro greens and herbs are baby versions of the regular size plant and are usually more tender with a very subtle flavor. If you cannot obtain micro greens, pick some of the smaller sprigs from larger size greens, such as the leaves on the inner stalk of celery, or the tiniest leaf on a stem of cilantro.

Tribal Wild Salmon Belly and Lobster Consommé

The belly of most edible animals is often the tastiest and most tender. Bacon, for example, comes from the belly of the hog. The salmon, important to Native American cuisine, is no exception. The relish made from the salmon belly is like a ceviche, and the consommé, which you can make ahead of time, is heated and poured over the relish at table.

Lobster Consommé

Put the lobster stock into a large pot and while it is cold; stir in the egg whites. Add the vegetables and chopped seafood, stir, and bring to a simmering boil. The egg whites form a "raft" that coagulates around the chopped vegetables and fish. After 1 hour of simmering, what remains is the clarified stock. Remove this raft and strain the consommé through a sieve lined with a coffee filter. Cool and store until ready to serve. Then heat and pour over the relish at table (see below).

Salmon Belly Relish

1. Sauté the shallots, garlic, and roasted corn in oil. Deglaze the pan with white wine.

2. In a mixing bowl, mix the sautéed vegetables together with the salmon belly, lobster coral, bean puree, pasilla, chives, and lime juice. Add salt and pepper to taste.

To Serve

Place the relish in a ring mold in the center of a wide dinner bowl. Remove the mold and pour the lobster consommé around the relish. Garnish with the micro chervil.

Serves 6

○○○

Chef O'Dowd Notes: Lobster shells make a marvelous stock, richer than other fish stock, so whenever you serve lobster, save the shells. Boil them with some aromatics and store the stock in your freezer for future use. Lobster coral, also called roe, is a delicacy and available in some fish markets.

○○○

3 quarts lobster stock (see Chef's Note)

4 egg whites

1 small onion, coarsely chopped

1 leek, cleaned and coarsely chopped

1 carrot, peeled and coarsely chopped

2 stalks of celery, coarsely chopped

1/2 pound cod fillet, coarsely chopped

1/2 pound shrimp, shells on, coarsely chopped

2 tablespoons minced shallots

2 teaspoons minced garlic

1 cup roasted corn

2 tablespoons canola oil

1 cup white wine

2 cups diced salmon belly (about a pound)

2 teaspoons lobster coral (see Chef's Note)

4 tablespoons cooked and pureed brown tepary beans (see Glossary)

2 tablespoons cooked minced pasilla chile (see Glossary)

2 tablespoons chopped chives

4 teaspoons fresh lime juice

Salt and pepper to taste

A few sprigs of micro chervil for garnish

Chilled Sixty-Day Sweet Corn Soup

6 ears yellow corn, roasted

2 tablespoons canola oil (approximate)

2 stalks celery, roughly chopped

1 onion, roughly chopped

1 leek, roughly chopped

2 shallots, chopped fine

1 tablespoon minced garlic

1 sprig fresh thyme

4 quarts chicken stock

3 cups heavy cream

1 teaspoon Tabasco

½ lemon, juiced

Salt and pepper to taste

Sixty-day corn is just what it says: corn that grows in sixty days rather than the longer period required by most types. This is a variety that is adapted to the arid climate and has a smaller stalk and white kernels. It is available from the Tohono O'odham farmers in southern Arizona. At Kai this tasty soup is sometimes served as an amuse bouche before dinner and topped with a bit of Mexican crema (similar to crème fraîche) and caviar. It is also delicious as is with huitlacoche biscotti (recipe on page 36).

1. Roast and shuck the corn and set aside.

2. In a large pot, sweat the vegetables with the garlic and thyme in the oil. Add the shucked corn. Once the vegetables are all coated with oil, deglaze the pot with the chicken stock. Cook over medium heat until the stock is reduced by half.

3. In another pan, reduce the cream by one-quarter.

4. Combine the cream and the soup and puree in a blender. Strain through a fine sieve. Adjust the seasoning with Tabasco, lemon juice, salt, and pepper. Chill and serve.

Serves 6

From the Oceans and Streams: Fish Entrees

The native people have been fishing the waters of the American continent for thousands of years and developing ways to prepare fish from the oceans, rivers, streams, and lakes. While there is no seacoast in the Sonoran Desert, the Gila River and its tributaries were once a source of fish. Native people used smoking and drying to preserve fish, while people from other parts of the world, such as Europe, used salting. Over the centuries the native people of the Northwest developed hot smoking to such an art that today's chefs and foodies are learning to do it, too. The heat cooks the meat and the smoke makes it flavorful. This method creates a drier, firmer fish.

Alder, which was abundant in the Northwest, is the traditional wood used for hot-smoking, but other woods including apple, maple, and mesquite are also used. Cedar planking is an old method of cooking that imparts flavor into salmon, halibut, and many other types of fish. At Kai those methods are employed with contemporary flourishes. As much as possible the chefs use fish from native fisheries, such as from the Lummi in Washington State, and fish is also prepared with land-based traditions such as fry bread.

◉◉◉◉◉◉◉◉◉◉◉◉◉◉◉◉◉◉◉◉◉

Butter-Basted Lobster Tail on Fry Bread with Avocado Mousse and Red and Yellow Teardrop Tomato Salsa

Native fry bread pairs well here with the spicy flavors of the Southwest and the sweet Maine lobster. You can prepare the bread, salsa, mousse, and vinaigrette ahead of time. This is a first course at Kai, but it would also make a terrific lunch or brunch dish.

Avocado Mousse

This is more like a pudding than a traditional mousse, and this recipe will make a bit more than you need for 4 servings, depending on the size of the avocados.

Put the avocados, jalapeño, and cilantro into a mixer and puree until smooth. Add the lemon and lime juices into the mixture. In thirds, add the cream cheese, occasionally scraping the sides of the bowl. Once the cream cheese is blended in, season with the chili powder, salt, and pepper. Refrigerate until ready to use.

2 avocados, pitted and peeled
1 jalapeño pepper
$\frac{1}{2}$ bunch fresh cilantro, leaves only
$\frac{1}{2}$ lemon, juiced
$\frac{1}{2}$ lime, juiced
6 ounces cream cheese, softened
$\frac{1}{2}$ teaspoon Santa Cruz chili powder
Salt and pepper to taste

Butter-Basted Lobster Tail

1. Preheat the oven to 350 degrees.
2. In a sauté pan, bring the water to a boil. Turn the heat to low and slowly stir in the butter until fully incorporated. Continue stirring until you have an emulsified sauce.
3. Place the cleaned lobster tails, meat exposed, onto a roasting pan and ladle the butter sauce over the lobster to cover. Sprinkle the fresh herbs and salt and pepper over the tails. Roast until completely cooked through, about 5 to 7 minutes.
4. Sauté the corn kernels in the oil until warm; season with salt and pepper.

2 tablespoons water
$\frac{1}{2}$ pound butter
4 lobster tails
1 tablespoon chopped chives
1 tablespoon chopped cilantro
Salt and pepper to taste
2 tablespoons canola oil
1 cup corn kernels
4 pieces Third-Generation Fry Bread (page 31)
1 cup Avocado Mousse
1 cup Red and Yellow Teardrop Tomato Salsa (page 111)
$\frac{1}{2}$ cup Golden Tomato Vinaigrette (page 104)

To Serve

Put about ¼ cup of corn kernels on each piece of fry bread. Follow this with the avocado mousse and the salsa. Place the lobster tail on top and drizzle some of the vinaigrette over each one.

Serve this with a dry white Burgundy wine with mineral accents, such as Olivier Leflaive "Les Folatieres," Puligny-Montrachet '04 to balance the buttery lobster and strong fruit flavors from the tomatoes.

Serves 4

Caramelized Red Mullet and Quinoa with Rhubarb Chutney

This is the Kai version of comfort food, a take on milk and cereal. Quinoa is a grain used by ancient Aztecs and in recent years has been discovered by foodies everywhere. At Kai this dish has a spicy coconut milk flavor from the Coco Lopez liqueur and the ginger and curry fumet.

Mullet is a small fish and cooks very quickly. The heat from the broiler will caramelize the skin of the fish, but you can also do this on the grill with the skin-side down. (You can also use bass or white fish, even halibut for this dish.) You will need three fillets per serving; six mullet will give you twelve fillets. Pour the fumet over the dish at table.

2 tablespoons canola oil

¼ cup chopped garlic

½ cup chopped shallots

½ stalk of lemongrass, chopped

¼ cup chopped leeks

½ cup peeled and chopped fresh ginger

1 tablespoon black peppercorns

½ tablespoon coriander seeds

½ bottle sake (about 2 cups)

¼ cup dried, crushed Kaffir lime leaves

1 quart fish fumet (see Chef's Note)

¼ tablespoon green curry paste (see Shopping Guide)

1 8-ounce can coconut milk

1½ tablespoons Coco Lopez liqueur

1 pinch bonito flakes

Salt and pepper to taste

Lime juice to taste

Fumet of Young Ginger and Green Curry–Infused Coconut

In a saucepan sweat the garlic, shallots, lemongrass, leeks, ginger, peppercorns, and coriander in canola oil. Deglaze the pan with sake, add the Kaffir lime leaves, and reduce by half. Add the fish fumet and simmer for 20 minutes, then whisk in the green curry paste. Simmer for another 20 minutes. Add the coconut milk, Coco Lopez, and bonito flakes and simmer for 10 minutes, then strain. Adjust the seasoning with salt and pepper and lime juice. Keep warm.

Makes 1 quart

⊙⊙

Chef O'Dowd Notes: Fish fumet is a classic rendition of fish stock. Fish heads and bones are cooked in water with various herbs, seasonings, and white wine. This broth is strained, boiled again, simmered, and reduced again and again to a glacé with intense flavor. Fumet can be used to flavor sauces, or it can be diluted again and used for braising and poaching. It is not too difficult to make, but it is available in fine gourmet stores.

⊙⊙

Quinoa and Red Mullet

1. Soak the dates (dried or fresh) for about 20 minutes in enough water to cover them plus a teaspoon of fresh lemon juice. Drain the dates and grill them on a clean, oiled grill on medium heat for a few minutes on each side. (The water will evaporate and the fruit will begin to caramelize.) Cool, chop, and set aside.

2. Season the fillets with salt and pepper. Place them skin-side up under the broiler for about 4 to 5 minutes.

3. Put the fillets in a warm sauté pan and add the chia seeds, plantago seeds, chopped shallots, and dates. Deglaze with fish stock or water and cook over medium heat until the seeds "bloom" and double in size while they become moist.

To Serve

Mold about ¼ cup of the quinoa in the middle of each serving bowl. Stack 3 filets per serving on top and top the fish with the chutney. Sprinkle dried cherries around the bowl. Fill some serving cups or small pitchers with the warm fumet. Pour the fumet over the dish tableside.

Serve with Chablis such as Joseph Drouhin '05. The high acidity, crisp fruit, and mineral notes help frame the flavors of the coconut fumet without battling the flavors of the mullet.

Serves 4

½ cup dates

1 teaspoon lemon juice

12 red mullet fillets

Salt and pepper

¼ cup chia seeds (see Shopping Guide)

¼ cup plantago seeds (see Shopping Guide)

1 teaspoon finely chopped shallots

½ cup fish stock or water

1 cup quinoa, cooked according to package instructions

1 cup Rhubarb Chutney (page 112)

1 tablespoon dried cherries for garnish

Cedar-Wrapped Tribal Black Cod with Potato and Leek Confit and Lobster–Tepary Bean Relish

The native people of the Northwest have a long tradition of slow-roasting fresh-caught salmon and other fish on cedar planks above their fire pits. The natural oils and moisture of the cedar infuse the flavor into the fish. Today, we can buy cedar papers to impart this special flavor to the food more easily and quickly. At Kai cedar papers along with some dried seaweed sheets (nori) are used to roll both the fish and potatoes and leeks into cylinders (like large sushi rolls) tied with leek "ribbons" before grilling. It is a perfect match for the fresh and spicy flavors of the lobster-tepary relish. You can simmer a 2½ pound Maine lobster in a broth of wine, onions, fennel, leek, meyer lemon, and peppercorns ahead of time (five minutes for the first pound and three minutes for each additional pound). An alternative is to buy already cooked lobster meat from your fishmonger. Make the relish first (you can refrigerate the leftover for future use), and grill the fish just before serving.

Cold-Water Lobster–Tepary Bean Relish

1 cup white tepary beans, cooked

1 cup brown tepary beans, cooked

1 cup roasted corn kernels

½ cup finely diced yellow bell pepper

¼ cup finely diced poblano pepper

¼ cup finely diced piquillo peppers

2 cups diced cooked lobster meat

1 tablespoon chopped cilantro

Pima Citrus-Vanilla Juice Marinade (page 105)

¼ cup extra-virgin olive oil

¼ cup avocado oil

Sea salt and freshly cracked pepper to taste

In a bowl, mix the beans, vegetables, and lobster meat. Add the chopped cilantro, Citrus-Vanilla Juice, and both oils. Finish with sea salt and fresh cracked pepper. Keep in the refrigerator until ready to use.

Cedar-Wrapped Tribal Black Cod with Potato and Leek Confit

1. Soak the cedar papers in water for at least 2 hours.

2. Marinate the cod in the Chili-Soy Marinade.

3. In a saucepan heat the rendered duck fat, and confit the potatoes until cooked through, about 15 minutes. Strain and reserve. Then repeat the same confit process in another pan with the leeks, which take about 5 to 7 minutes to cook through.

4. Preheat the oven to 350 degrees.

5. Place six wet cedar sheets on the table, and layer a sheet of nori onto each one. Then place a marinated piece of cod in the middle and shingle the confited potatoes on both sides of the cod. Layer evenly a small amount of the confited leeks on top of the cod and follow with layers of pea shoots and cilantro leaves. Roll each of the filled sheets up like sushi rolls and fasten them with the ribbons of blanched leek.

6. Place the rolls into a sauté pan with a bit of water and roast them uncovered for about 15 minutes in the oven.

To Serve

Line each serving dish with some sea beans or shredded nori or other seaweed. Place a roll on each plate. Make two or three diagonal slices in each roll to expose the inside. At the table, spoon some of the lobster-tepary relish onto each dish.

Pair this dish with a Sancerre such as Comte Lafond '04. The wine's bright fruit is a wonderful addition to the delicate flavors of this dish.

Serves 6

6 cedar papers (see Chef's Note)

6 five-ounce portions of skinless cod fillet

Chili Jam Marinade (page 105)

1 quart rendered duck fat

½ pound fingerling potatoes, sliced lengthwise

1 leek, cleaned and sliced

6 sheets nori

Pea shoots and cilantro leaves

Leek greens, blanched and sliced on the bias

Sea beans or shredded seaweed, optional

◎◎

Chef Strong Notes: Cedar papers are available in specialty food stores and online in packs of four or eight, for about $10 for the larger one. Be sure to get the ones made of natural Western red cedar for best flavor. They can be used for seafood, veggies, fruit, even cheese. You can use them in the oven or over hot grill grates, and the food will steam to perfection inside the papers.

◎◎

Spiked Hamachi with Saguaro Gelée and Pomegranate-Ginger Spritzer

Hamachi is the big fleshy collar around the nape of a large fish such as yellowtail tuna or salmon. This part of the fish is very flavorful. Sometimes it is lightly smoked, and sometimes the skin is crisped up like cracklings. At Kai this delicious part of the tuna is served on a bed of saguaro gelée with the spritzer poured over it. Make the gelée ahead of time.

Saguaro Gelée

2 cups mineral water

5 sheets gelatin (see Chef's Note on page 40)

½ gallon blood orange juice

½ cup orange juice

½ ounce saguaro syrup (see Shopping Guide)

1. Bloom (soften) the gelatin sheets in the cold water for 10 minutes. Allow to open and become soft to the touch. Set aside for 5 to 10 minutes.

2. In a saucepan, heat up the orange juices and saguaro syrup. Remove the gelatin sheets from the cold water and drain away excess water on a towel. Add the bloomed gelatin to the juice and syrup mixture and dissolve. Pour the mix into a layer cake pan and allow it to cool.

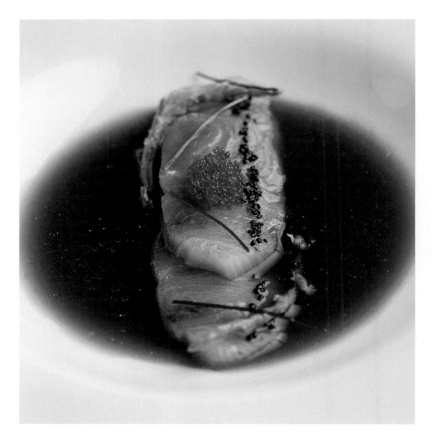

Pomegranate-Ginger Spritzer

Grate some fresh ginger, wrap it in cheesecloth, and squeeze out some juice. Mix together everything but the ginger ale. Set aside.

Fresh ginger
1 ounce blood orange juice
1 ounce pomegranate juice
1 ounce cranberry juice
1 ounce ginger ale

Spiked Hamachi

1. Thinly slice the well-chilled hamachi and set aside.

2. Add the ginger ale to the spritzer mix and pour into four shot glasses.

3. Pipe the Saguaro Gelée in a straight line across each serving bowl. Layer 3 pieces of Hamachi on top of the gelée in each bowl. Garnish the middle of the hamachi with a generous teaspoon of the caviar and place 2 pomegranate seeds on each side of the caviar. Place 2 sprigs of sea beans on each side. At tableside pour 1 spritzer over each dish.

Serves 4

4 ounces thinly sliced hamachi (yellowtail tuna)
1 teaspoon tobiko caviar (see Chef's Note)
16 pomegranate seeds
16 sprigs of sea beans (optional)
1/2 cup Saguaro Gelée
1 cup Pomegranate-Ginger Spritzer

◎◎

Chef O'Dowd Notes: Tobiko caviar is the roe harvested from flying fish and, because it keeps well, it has become popular to season this roe with different flavors and coloring. For example, the yellow tobiko is typically a ginger flavor; light green is wasabi flavor. The natural color is orange, and the roe is slightly sweet with salty overtones. It has a crunchy texture and is an ideal garnish. It will keep in the freezer and is available in Asian and gourmet stores.

◎◎

From the Prairie and the Sky: Meat, Game, Poultry Entrees

The mountains and plains sheltered buffalo, deer, elk, wild turkey, and other game important to Native Americans for centuries. The people made use not only of the meat, but of the hides and antlers. Small game like ducks, geese, and grouse were plentiful along rivers and streams, and quail and rabbits were common in the desert.

Once again meat is being raised naturally, the way it was done in the time of the native people. Much of the free-range, grass-fed meat the native people once ate is available once again. Buffalo—or correctly, American Bison—is a popular alternative to beef. The buffalo cooked at Kai is from the Cheyenne River Sioux Tribe and is always on the menu. In addition to venison and elk, the beef and pork at Kai are the American-raised version of the Japanese Kobe and Korubuta.

◉◎◉◎◉◎◉◎◉◎◉◎◉◎◉◎◉◎◉◎◉

Skillet-Seared Prairie Squab Breast with Oxtail
Merquez Sausage Frittata Española 72
Pecan-Crusted Colorado Rack of Lamb with Recado Rub
and Cornbread Pudding 75
Grilled Tenderloin of Buffalo with Smoked Corn Puree,
Chorizo Scarlet Runner Beans, and Cholla Buds 77
Grilled Elk Chop with Truffle, Gila River Eggplant Caviar,
and Saguaro Seed Phyllo Dough Crisps 80
Korobuta Pork Tenderloin Rubbed with Toasted Ground Coffee
and Pueblo Hatch Chiles with Dried Fruit Crostini and Plum Chutney 82
Dry-Aged American Kobe Beef Tenderloin with Desert Succotash
and Golden Raisin Compote 84

Skillet-Seared Prairie Squab Breast with Oxtail

Skillet-Seared Prairie Squab Breast with Oxtail Merquez Sausage Frittata Española

The components of this dish can all be made ahead, leaving the squab preparation and assembly for just before serving. The squab should marinate in the herbs at least overnight, but ideally for about five days because it is a way of preserving that adds an herbal essence to the delicate flavor of this dark meat. Your steps should be to first marinate the squab, then prepare the pulled oxtail meat, then the frittata, and finally the squab.

Squab Marinade

Mix the shallots, garlic, and herbs with the olive oil and pour over the squab. If using the whole squab, separate the breasts from the body. Keep in a covered bowl or plastic bag in the refrigerator and marinate for five days or at least overnight in the refrigerator.

½ cup minced shallots
½ cup minced roasted garlic
Sprigs of fresh thyme, rosemary, and lavender
1 to 1½ cups olive oil
4 squab (breasts or whole)

Braised Oxtail

Oxtail is no longer from an ox, but from veal or beef. This bony cut holds great flavor but is very tough, so long, slow braising is necessary. When the meat is pulled from the bones, it is extremely tender.

Cheesecloth and butcher's twine for sachet
½ bunch thyme
2 fresh bay leaves
¼ cup black peppercorns
1 cup all-purpose flour
Salt and pepper
5 oxtails cut into 3-inch pieces
¼ cup canola oil (approximate)
3 carrots, peeled and chopped
2 onions, chopped
3 celery stalks, chopped
1½ dry ancho chiles, seeded
½ mojo rojo chile, seeded
2 heads garlic, cut in half
½ gallon veal stock
1 quart chicken stock

1. Preheat the oven to 250 degrees.

2. Wrap the thyme, bay leaves, and peppercorns in cheesecloth and tie with the twine to make a sachet, or bouquet garni, and set aside.

3. In a mixing bowl, season the flour with salt and pepper. Dredge the oxtail pieces in the seasoned flour and sear in some oil in a large hot sauté pan. Remove and set aside. In the same pan caramelize the vegetables, garlic, and chiles.

4. Put the caramelized vegetables and the oxtails into a roasting pan. Add the bouquet garni and veal and chicken stock to cover. Cover the pan and braise in the oven at 250 degrees for 4 hours or until the oxtail is very tender and falling off the bone. Remove the oxtail from the pan and pull the meat from the bone.

5. Strain the braising liquid into a saucepan and reduce by half. Strain again through a fine sieve and adjust seasoning with salt and pepper. Combine with the meat and set aside in the refrigerator until ready to use.

Serves 4

Frittata Española

In addition to the seared prairie squab, this spicy frittata pairs well with any poultry or game. Unlike a traditional frittata that is made in a skillet, this one is baked on a sheet pan. The fideo pasta is sometimes known as Mexican pasta and comes in coiled strands. It is toasted before cooking in liquid, which gives the dish a bit of crunch.

1. Preheat the oven to 350 degrees and grease a sheet pan with the butter.

2. In a large saucepan, sweat the onion and garlic in the oil over medium heat until translucent. Add the sausage and cook until brown. Then add the pasta and toast until golden brown. Add the saffron, chili powder, and smoked paprika; mix well while continuing to cook. Add tomato, tomato juice, cilantro, and enough chicken stock to cover all the ingredients. Cook until heated through and add salt and pepper to taste. Remove the pan from the heat and allow it to cool thoroughly before adding the eggs. Break the eggs into a bowl and whisk together before adding to the pan with the cooled mixture.

3. Pour the mixture onto the greased baking sheet and cook at 350 degrees for about 30 minutes, or until the frittata is firm to the touch. Remove and allow to cool.

Serves 4 or 6

1 tablespoon butter

2 tablespoons canola oil

1 yellow onion, diced small

1½ tablespoons minced garlic

2 lamb merquez sausages, diced

½ pound fideo pasta

1 saffron thread

1 tablespoon chili powder (preferably Santa Cruz brand)

1 tablespoon smoked paprika

1 plum tomato, diced small

1 cup tomato juice

1 teaspoon fresh cilantro, chopped fire

2 cups (approximate) chicken stock

Salt and pepper to taste

12 eggs

⊙⊙⊙

Chef O'Dowd Notes: Merquez is a spicy lamb sausage used in Moroccan cuisine. With its cumin, garlic, chili, and cayenne, it makes a tasty accompaniment to eggs. There really is no substitute for this with the Frittata Española.

⊙⊙⊙

4 squab breasts marinated
   in Squab Marinade
Salt and fresh cracked
   pepper
4 tablespoons canola oil
Frittata Española
1 cup (approximate)
   Tomatillo Mud (page 111)
1 cup (approximate) pulled
   Braised Oxtail meat
1/2 cup water or chicken
   stock
Verdologas (purslane)
   sprigs for garnish
Huitlacoche Mojo (page
   106)
Piquillo Pepper Sauce
   (page 108)

Skillet-Seared Prairie Squab

Squab is a young pigeon that has never flown, so it is very tender. Be sure not to overcook it.

1. Preheat the oven to 350 degrees.

2. Remove the squab from the marinade and pat dry with paper towels. Season with salt and pepper. For each squab, heat 1 tablespoon oil in a small sauté pan over medium heat and place the squab skin-side down. Sear until the skin is golden brown and crisp. Turn it over and sear meat-side down. When all the squabs are seared, place them in a larger pan and finish in the oven until medium-rare, about 3 to 5 minutes.

3. Heat the frittata in the oven at the same time, also for 3 to 5 minutes. Then cut the frittata into circles, squares, or other shapes for individual portions.

4. Warm the Tomatillo Mud.

5. Heat the pulled Braised Oxtail in a little chicken stock or water, season with salt and pepper, and set aside.

To Serve

Pool a spoonful of the Tomatillo Mud in the middle of each serving bowl. Place a piece of the Frittata Española on top of the mud. Evenly spread the oxtail on the frittata and place 3 to 4 sprigs of verdolagas on top of that. Set the squab breast on top. Finish with dots of the huitlacoche and piquillo sauces.

Choose a light red wine for this dish such as a Pinot Noir or a Rioja such as Conde de Valdemar, Gran Reserva '97, a medium-bodied wine with rustic fruit flavors.

Pecan-Crusted Colorado Rack of Lamb
with Recado Rub and Cornbread Pudding

This is a favorite way to serve Colorado lamb at Kai and it is so popular, it is never removed from the menu. This recipe will work with lamb loin as well as the rack. The Recado Rub is a wet mole developed at Kai with heritage ingredients from Native Seeds/SEARCH. This rich, flavorful lamb is a perfect match for the Cornbread Pudding on page 34. Serve it with asparagus spears.

1 cup pecan pieces

1 cup pumpkin seeds

2 dried ancho chiles, seeded, stemmed, and torn

3 tablespoons ground cinnamon

1 tablespoon ground cumin

3 tablespoons Santa Cruz chili powder

4 chipotles in adobo, seeded (see Shopping Guide)

1 cup raisins

1/2 cup brown sugar

1 4-ounce can orange juice concentrate

1/2 cup balsamic vinegar

1 cup Queen Creek or other virgin olive oil

1 cup mineral water

2 racks of lamb

Recado Rub

Salt and pepper to taste

1 cup ground pecans

1 1/2 cups Kai Native Seeds/ SEARCH Mole (page 107)

Cornbread Pudding (page 34)

18 to 24 blanched asparagus spears

Recado Rub for Lamb

Toast the pecans and pumpkin seeds together in a heavy skillet. Add ancho chiles, cinnamon, cumin, and chili powder, and toast lightly. Allow to cool, then grind the mixture in a food processor along with the chipotles, raisins, brown sugar, orange juice concentrate, and balsamic vinegar. Puree until smooth and add olive oil in a slow stream. Thin the mixture with mineral water until it has a slightly loose appearance.

Makes 1 quart

Rack of Lamb

1. Preheat oven to 375 degrees.

2. Most butchers will clean the exposed bones of the rack of lamb, but to do it yourself, remove the meat from the bones and wipe down the bones with a damp cloth. Cut each rack in half, and season with salt and pepper. Rub generously with the Recado Rub and roll the meat in the ground pecans, or pat them around it.

3. Roast the lamb on a wire rack in a roasting pan until desired temperature for medium-rare, about 130 to 140 degrees on an instant-read thermometer. This will take about 10 to 12 minutes. Let the lamb rest for 10 minutes before serving. Cut into individual chops.

4. Warm up the mole in a small pan on the stove.

To Serve

Make a pool of the Kai Native Seeds/SEARCH Mole on each plate. Cut the Cornbread Pudding into individual squares, triangles, or circles, any shape that seems appealing. Put a piece on the mole and lean the lamb chop against it. Arrange 3 asparagus spears on each plate. (Alternatively, you can omit the pool of mole and simply drizzle some around the plate.)

Serve with a Cabernet Sauvignon such as Solaris "Reserve," Napa '02, or a Chateau Palmer, Margaux '03, which has an earthy backbone but more elegance than most Bordeaux.

Serves 6 to 8

Grilled Tenderloin of Buffalo with Smoked Corn Puree, Chorizo Scarlet Runner Beans, and Cholla Buds

The Cheyenne River Sioux in North Dakota breed and raise grass-fed buffalo for the growing market of people who appreciate its flavor and texture. Buffalo meat is lower in cholesterol, leaner, and a bit sweeter than beef. Cook it quickly—and never well done—for the best flavor and texture. For this recipe, the buffalo meat is marinated before cooking. Prepare the beans and corn puree first, then grill the meat. This is delicious served with caramelized mushrooms and haricots verts.

Chorizo Scarlet Runner Beans

Scarlet runners are big purple beans with black flecks. They have a creamy texture when cooked, and remarkable flavor. Those used at Kai are grown from heritage seeds from Native Seeds/SEARCH. This dish of beans and sausage is a sort of hash or chili that suits the tender sweetness of the buffalo and smokiness of the corn puree.

1½ cups scarlet runner
   beans, soaked overnight
1 quart mineral water
½ head garlic
½ bunch fresh thyme
1 teaspoon canola oil
1 small yellow onion, diced
   small
1½ poblano chiles, roasted,
   peeled, diced small
1 jalapeño chile, seeded,
   finely diced
1¼ pounds ground
   Mexican chorizo
2 tablespoons chopped
   garlic
⅓ to ½ cup ketchup
½ cup chicken stock
Sea salt and cracked black
   pepper to taste

1. In a large saucepan, boil the scarlet runner beans in salted mineral water with the garlic and thyme until fully cooked, about 1 hour. Cool and reserve.

2. Sauté the onion and chiles until soft. Add the chorizo and fully cook. Stir in the chopped garlic, ketchup, and beans. Pour in the chicken stock and reduce the heat to simmer for about 15 minutes. Season with salt and pepper.

Serves 4 to 6

Smoked Corn Puree

6 ears of yellow corn,
  roasted and smoked
1 to 2 cups mesquite chips
2 tablespoons canola oil
1 stalk celery, roughly
  chopped
1/2 leek, rough chopped
1 shallot, chopped
1 potato, peeled and
  roughly chopped
1/2 large or 1 small onion,
  roughly chopped
1 teaspoon chopped garlic
1/2 bunch fresh thyme
1/2 gallon chicken stock
3 cups heavy cream
Sea salt and cracked black
  pepper to taste
1/2 teaspoon Tabasco
1/2 lemon, juiced

1. Roast the corn in a 350-degree oven in the husks for about 20 minutes. Allow to cool and then shuck and prepare to smoke the corn in mesquite chips.

2. Line a large sauté pan with the mesquite chips. Place the corn in a perforated pan (slightly smaller than the one with the chips) and set it on top of the chips. Loosely cover with a piece of foil and set the stove to a low-to-medium heat. Smoke the corn for about 5 minutes, being careful not to over-smoke. Cut the kernels from the cob and reserve both corn and cobs.

3. In a large sauté pan, sweat the vegetables, garlic, and thyme in oil. Add the corn and the cobs. Deglaze with chicken stock and cook over medium heat until the stock is reduced by half. At the same time, in another pan, reduce the cream by a quarter. Once the stock has reduced, discard the corncobs and puree the vegetables in a blender with the heavy cream. Strain through a fine sieve. Adjust the seasoning with salt, pepper, Tabasco, and lemon juice to taste. It should have the consistency of a thin puree, or lobster bisque.

Makes 1 quart

Grilled Buffalo

1. Marinate the buffalo in the General Herb Marinade for 2 to 4 hours. When ready to cook, remove the buffalo from the marinade and season with salt and fresh cracked black pepper. Grill about 8 to 12 minutes for medium-rare, the best way to serve buffalo, which is very lean and cooks quickly. Let the meat rest.

2. Heat the Smoked Corn Puree and Chorizo Scarlet Runner Beans.

3. Sauté the haricots verts and cholla buds together in the canola oil.

4. Heat the caramelized mushroom slices in a sauté pan.

5. Toss the grilled piquillo pepper slices and squash blossoms together as for a salad.

To Serve

Spoon a pool of the corn puree in the middle of each large dinner bowl. Spoon some of the chorizo runner beans onto the puree and sprinkle 4 cholla buds around the edge of the pool. Top each mound with 6 haricots verts. Top those with a small amount of the piquillo-squash blossom salad and place the buffalo tenderloin on top of that. To finish, spoon a small amount of caramelized mushrooms on top of the buffalo and drizzle saguaro syrup around the plate.

This pairs well with a Shiraz such as Wyndham "Show Reserve," southeastern Australia '04 or Penfold's Grange '01, big-bodied wines with high tannin and peppery spice to complement the chorizo.

Serves 6

6 8-ounce pieces of buffalo tenderloin, cleaned and trimmed
General Herb Marinade (page 105)
1 cup Smoked Corn Puree
1½ cups Chorizo Scarlet Runner Beans
1 tablespoon canola oil
36 blanched haricots verts
24 cholla buds (page 90)
1 cup mushroom mix for garnish (page 116)
½ to ¾ cup thinly sliced grilled piquillo peppers
8 to 10 squash blossoms, thinly sliced, for garnish
¼ cup saguaro syrup (see Shopping Guide)

Grilled Elk Chop with Truffle, Gila River Eggplant Caviar, and Saguaro Seed Phyllo Dough Crisps

Elk was once considered a tough form of venison, but it is becoming popular as farmers find better ways to raise this animal. It is lower in fat and cholesterol than beef. It is also very expensive, and so far most of it is imported from New Zealand.

Gila River Eggplant Caviar
The children at the Gila Crossing grow this eggplant for Kai. It is a very fresh, tender, medium-sized eggplant. It is called "caviar" because when the seeds show through the quenelle of fluffy mousse-like texture, they look a bit like caviar.

2 eggplants, cut in half

2 cups kosher salt

1/4 cup olive oil

Salt and fresh cracked black pepper

1 bunch fresh thyme

1 head garlic, cut in half

Juice of 1 lemon

1. Cut the eggplants in half and press them flesh-side down into the kosher salt for about 20 minutes to remove some of the bitterness. (Put a sheet pan over them and weight it down with some cast-iron pans.) Rinse the eggplant and toss with olive oil, salt, and pepper.

2. In a pre-heated 375-degree oven, roast the eggplant with the thyme and head of garlic until soft. Let cool, peel, and mash.

3. Scoop out the eggplant pulp and puree in a food processor with 1 tablespoon roasted garlic and the lemon juice. Slowly add the olive oil, and season with salt and pepper to finish.

Saguaro Seed Phyllo Dough Crisps
When done, these crisps will be layered with caramelized mushrooms to form savory Napoleons.

2 tablespoons saguaro seeds (see Shopping Guide)

2 tablespoons ground pepitas (pumpkin seeds)

2 tablespoons ground fennel seeds

1 package phyllo dough, thawed

1 cup clarified butter

1/2 cup puffed amaranth (see Glossary)

Salt and cracked black pepper

1. Preheat the oven to 375 degrees and line a small sheet pan with parchment paper.

2. In a dry sauté pan, toast all the seeds. Keep the saguaro seeds whole, but grind the pepitas and fennel seeds into a fine powder in a coffee grinder. Set aside.

3. Lay one sheet of the thawed phyllo dough on a clean surface, then cover the rest with a lightly damp cloth to prevent the phyllo from drying out. Brush heavily with clarified butter. Lightly dust with ground fennel and pepitas, and sprinkle on some saguaro seeds. Repeat this process four more times, giving you five layers of phyllo dough.

4. On top layer, sprinkle the puffed amaranth and season with salt and pepper. Line a half sheet pan with parchment paper and place the phyllo on it and top with another piece of paper. Weight it down with two half sheet pans. Bake at 375 degrees until golden brown. Let cool and cut into perfect squares.

Elk Chop

1. Marinate the rack of elk in the herb marinade for 2 to 4 hours. Season with salt and pepper, and grill until medium-rare. Slice the rack of elk into individual chops.

2. Sprinkle the exposed meat with a finishing sea salt such as Maldon.

3. Slice black truffle on top to garnish.

To Serve

Use rectangular serving dishes for a handsome presentation. Using a teaspoon to shape a quenelle, place some eggplant caviar on one side and garnish it by forming a twig with two slivers of the yucca. Place the elk chop lengthwise in the center, with the bone end against the eggplant. Shave some truffle over the chop. At the other end of the dish, layer a few phyllo crisps with chopped mushrooms to form a Napoleon.

This dish pairs with a big-bodied wine with high tannins, such as Girard "Artistry," Napa '04.

1 rack of elk
1 cup General Herb
  Marinade (page 105)
Salt and pepper
Sea salt
Fresh black truffle (see
  Chef's Note)
Gila River Eggplant Caviar
Raw yucca slivers (cassava)
  for garnish
Saguaro Seed Phyllo Dough
  Crisps
Mushroom Mix for Garnish
  (page 116)

Chef O'Dowd Notes: There is nothing quite like the earthy perfume of black truffles, or "black diamonds" as they are often called. Truffle is a perfect partner for the elk, so try to prepare this dish when they are available. With an inexpensive truffle slicer from your kitchen gadget store, angle the (very expensive) truffle against the blade at a 45-degree angle for paper-thin slivers. It's best to use the truffle right away, but if you need to store it for a day or two in the fridge, bury it in a container with whole eggs or rice and cover tightly. Otherwise, everything in your fridge will smell like truffle—which is not bad, perhaps, but a waste.

Korobuta Pork Tenderloin Rubbed with Toasted Ground Coffee and Pueblo Hatch Chiles with Dried Fruit Crostini and Plum Chutney

The Kurobuta pork served at Kai comes from Snake River Farms, which raises the American version of the Japanese pork from black hogs. This lean meat is tender and juicy, darker in color than traditional pork, and has rich flavor. Because it contains less water, there is less weight loss after cooking. For this dish the tenderloin is rubbed with Kai's special dry mole combined with toasted ground "fair trade" coffee and pueblo Hatch chiles. At Kai this is served with a tian of rainbow chard leaves.

Dried Fruit Crostini

7 ounces quince paste

12 ounces dried fruit

12 cloves roasted garlic, smashed

4 ounces shallots, sweated

1 ounce chipotle puree

1/2 tablespoon cinnamon

1 1/4 bottle Martinelli or similar brand sparkling apple cider

1/2 ounce honey

6 eggs

1/2 loaf cranberry-walnut bread, sliced and diced small

1/2 round of sourdough bread, sliced and diced small

1 cup Mushroom Mix for Garnish (page 116)

1. Preheat the oven to 350 degrees.

2. In a bowl mix the quince paste, dried fruit, garlic, shallots, chipotle, and cinnamon into a paste. Add the sparkling cider, honey, and eggs, and mix thoroughly. Add the bread cubes and let sit in the refrigerator for about 45 minutes.

3. Line a sheet pan with parchment paper and butter it generously. Press the moist fruit and bread mixture into the sheet pan. Fill the pan up to the rim for a thick crostini. For a thinner crostini, use only enough of the mixture to go halfway up to the rim of the pan.

4. Bake for about 45 minutes or until crisp. (If making the thinner version, check in about 35 minutes.) Break into even pieces and make two or three layers with the mushrooms to form Napoleons.

Pork Tenderloin

1. Mix the Mole Dust dry rub and coffee together and reserve.

2. Using a very sharp knife, remove the silver skin from the pork tenderloin. This is the fine membrane that covers the meat; if it is not removed, the meat may curl during cooking. Roll the cleaned pork tenderloin in the dry rub, and sear the pork on all sides with olive oil in a small oven-proof sauté pan. Place the pan in a preheated 375-degree oven until desired temperature, about 17 minutes for medium-rare. Let rest for 5 minutes before serving; meanwhile prepare the rainbow chard as described on page 91.

To Serve

Slice the pork tenderloin into portion sizes, about 3 inches thick. Make some lines on each serving plate with the chutney. Place a slice of the pork in the center, a mound of chard on one side, and a crostini Napoleon on the other.

K Vitners "Boy," Grenache '06, a light–medium-bodied wine with delicate flavors, would be a good match for this dish.

Serves 4 to 6

1 cup Mole Dust (page 110)

1 cup ground "fair trade" coffee

1 tenderloin of pork

1 cup Plum Chutney (see page 113)

Tian of Rainbow Chard Leaves

Dry-Aged American Kobe Beef Tenderloin with Desert Succotash and Golden Raisin Compote

At Kai the Kobe beef is hung in a cooler for two weeks to dry-age. This tenderizes the meat and adds an intense earthy flavor. You can buy Kobe or other top quality dry-aged beef from a good butcher, but if you have a place where you can maintain a temperature between 40 and 50 degrees for up to two weeks, then try dry-aging it at home. At the butt end of the tenderloin, pierce a small hole to run the butcher's twine through for hanging.

The beef is rubbed with truffle oil before searing over high heat for a fabulous flavor. A Cabernet reduction, which you can make ahead, adds the finishing taste touch.

Cabernet Reduction

2 shallots, peeled and chopped

1 to 2 tablespoons canola oil

1 bottle port wine

$\frac{1}{2}$ bottle Cabernet Sauvignon

$\frac{1}{2}$ cup veal stock

In a saucepan sauté the shallots over medium heat until caramelized. Deglaze the pan with the Port, Cabernet, and veal stock. Reduce by two-thirds or until it begins to become syrupy; this takes about 30 minutes. Strain and reserve.

Beef Tenderloin

1. Clean any silver skin from the tenderloin and slice it into portions, about 3 inches thick. Drizzle each fillet with truffle oil to coat well. Season the fillets with sea salt and fresh black pepper.

2. In a hot sauté pan, sear the fillets on all sides and finish in a 375-degree oven. For such tender beef, rare to medium-rare is ideal and takes between 7 and 10 minutes. Sprinkle the meat with the cheese crumbles and put it under the broiler to caramelize for a minute. You can also do this with a brûlée torch if you have one.

To Serve

Paint some lines of Cabernet Reduction across each serving dish (or drizzle around the completed plate). Pool some compote in the center of each dish. Lay the meat across the plate and put some of the succotash alongside.

This dish pairs well with Cabernet and Bordeaux, and especially with Barolo or Barbaresco. Another choice is an old-world wine such as Chateau Montrose, St. Estephe '98, big-bodied and aggressive with high tannins.

Serves 6

1 dry-aged tenderloin of beef

6 tablespoons white truffle oil

Maldon sea salt and fresh cracked black pepper

6 tablespoons crumbled Cabrales cheese (see Chef's Note)

6 portions Desert Succotash (page 88)

1 cup (approximate) Golden Raisin Compote (page 112)

○○

Chef O'Dowd Notes: We use many types of sea salt at Kai (see page 114), and the best for this dish is Maldon, which has larger flakes than others and adds a bit of tangy crunch to the tender meat.

○○

○○

Chef Strong Notes: Cabrales is a blue cheese from Spain that is sometimes called "the meanest blue" because it is so sharp and spicy. This semisoft cheese has a granular texture and is made from cow's, sheep's, and goat's milk.

○○

From the Earth: Vegetable Side Dishes

Here are some of the popular vegetable sides that accompany entrees at Kai. As we have mentioned throughout this book, vegetables were a major part of the diet of the early people. Corn, of course, is very important, and it was used in various forms—including posole, or hominy, made from large kernels of dried corn soaked in lime to remove the hulls and plump them up. After simmering with other ingredients and seasonings, this is a versatile vegetable. Posole is also available canned. When using the canned variety, rinse and drain it before cooking.

At home you may want to match up some of these with your own favorites. There are one or two that are not part of any of the dishes in this book, but that we thought you might enjoy.

◎◎◎◎◎◎◎◎◎◎◎◎◎◎◎◎◎◎◎◎◎

Poscle and Desert Succotash

Posole and Desert Succotash

Corn, squash, and beans are the "three sisters" of Native American cuisine (see Chapter 1), and this trio is used in many ways. Here, local flavor is added with desert plants as well as huitlacoche, a corn fungus that was a great favorite of the ancient Aztecs. (Today some corn is grown just to harvest this delicacy.) Posole, or hominy, is dried corn used traditionally as a base for soup, but here it gives substance to the succotash for a perfect side dish served with mushrooms and asparagus and Dry-Aged American Kobe Beef Tenderloin (see page 84). It makes a great vegetable complement to any meal.

3 quarts mineral water

1 pound posole, soaked in water

4 nopales pads (nopalitas) (see Chef's Note)

1 cup diced pancetta

1 medium butternut squash, peeled and diced small

1 cup diced Vidalia onions

3 ears roasted corn, kernels removed

4 purple potatoes, julienne

1/2 cup huitlacoche

3 or 4 piquillo peppers, diced small

1 tablespoon roasted garlic

1 cup chicken stock

1 tablespoon Plugra butter

Few sprigs of fresh sage, chiffonade

1. Cook the soaked posole in 2 quarts mineral water until tender, then set aside to cool.

2. Peel the nopales, simmer in water until tender, cool, and dice. Set aside.

3. In a large sauté pan cook the pancetta over medium heat. Add the squash, onions, and posole and continue to cook until softened. Next, add the corn, potatoes, huitlacoche, peppers, garlic, and nopalitos. Continue cooking until ingredients are cooked through, about 10 minutes.

4. Stir in the chicken stock to deglaze the pan. Reduce the heat and cook another 5 or 6 minutes. Just before serving, add the butter and sage.

To Serve

To serve with a meat dish, place some of the succotash into a small ring mold, then unmold it alongside the meat. Rest some asparagus spears against the succotash for an elegant presentation.

Serves 6 to 8 as a side dish

○◎○

Chef Strong Notes: Nopales are the pads of the prickly pear. They have a tart flavor similar to green beans. Fresh pads can be found in Latino and some gourmet markets. Use a vegetable peeler to remove the skin, then simmer the pads in water until tender. Pickled nopalitas, already diced, are available in jars or cans.

○◎○

Pickled Local Squash

At Kai, these pickles are made with just-picked local summer squash. This relish will keep for weeks in the refrigerator, so you can use it with seafood, venison (page 41), and other dishes.

Mix the first 11 ingredients and pour over the diced squash. Refrigerate.

Serves 10 to 12 as side dish or more as a relish or garnish

2 cups apple cider vinegar
2 cups water
5 fresh parsley stems
10 to 12 sprigs fresh thyme
3 tablespoons coriander
1 tablespoon celery seed
2 tablespoons fennel seed
2 tablespoons black
   peppercorns
3/4 cup sugar
Salt to taste
1/4 cup rice wine vinegar
2 zucchini, de-seeded and
   diced small
2 yellow summer squash,
   seeded and diced small

Horseradish Dauphinoise Potatoes

This dish sometimes accompanies a New York filet mignon at Kai, but you can serve it with any red meat.

1. Preheat the oven to 350 degrees. Grease a baking pan and line it with parchment.
2. Peel the potatoes and make thin slices on a mandoline.
3. In a saucepan, reduce the cream with the prepared and fresh horseradish, garlic, and sprigs of thyme. Then strain and set aside.
4. In a large bowl, toss the potato slices with the reduced cream, thyme leaves, 1 pound of the cheese, and salt and pepper to taste.
5. Arrange one layer of potatoes in the bottom of the pan and sprinkle with some of the remaining cheese. Add another layer of potatoes and cheese and so on until the pan is about three-quarters full.
6. Pour the remaining cream over the top.
7. Bake uncovered for 45 minutes. Uncover and bake for an additional 15 minutes until browned.

Serves 10 to 12 as side dish

17 russet potatoes
4 cups heavy cream
3 tablespoons prepared
   horseradish
3 fresh horseradish, grated
1 head garlic, cut in half
Sprigs of thyme
Fresh thyme leaves (scraped
   from their stems)
1 1/2 pounds Gruyère, grated
Salt and pepper to taste

Cholla Buds

1 bag dried cholla buds (see Shopping Guide)
4 cups orange juice
Few sprigs fresh thyme
1 teaspoon chopped garlic
1 tablespoon butter
Salt and pepper

Cholla buds are from a cactus plant and are used a lot at Kai for various dishes, including rack of elk. The buds are available dried, so they can be used any time of year. This is the basic preparation for reconstituting the buds and making them ready to sauté or use cold in any number of dishes. Or simply sauté them with a bit of garlic and butter as a tasty side dish.

1. Place the first three ingredients in a saucepan and bring to a boil, then reduce heat and simmer for about 30 minutes until tender. Allow to cool, and look for any prickly needles still left in the buds.

2. Sauté the cholla buds in garlic and butter. Season to taste with salt and pepper.

Makes about 2 cups

Olive Oil–Marinated Grape Tomatoes

3 pints grape tomatoes, washed
1 head of garlic, cut in half
1 bunch thyme
2 cups olive oil to cover (approximate)

In this recipe the thyme, garlic, and olive oil create a lovely essence with the tart, sweet tomato. This is a form of confit (page 57).

Place the grape tomatoes, garlic, and thyme in a saucepan and cover with olive oil. On low heat, poach the tomatoes until tender, about 15 minutes. Cool in the olive oil to infuse the garlic and thyme flavors. To reheat, warm up in the oil over low heat.

Serves 6

Roasted Baby Beets

At Kai these roasted baby beets are often served with pork or duck. They are extremely versatile, and you can use them cold in salads, hot as a side dish, or as a garnish.

1. Preheat oven to 375 degrees.

2. Put the thyme, garlic, shallots, and bay leaves, into a roasting pan. Toss the beets with olive oil, salt, and pepper and place them on top of the aromatics in the pan. Cover with foil and roast until the beets are tender, about 45 to 60 minutes.

3. Allow the beets to cool until you can peel off the skin. Refrigerate.

Serves 6

1 bunch thyme

2 heads garlic, cut in half

6 shallots, chopped

3 bay leaves

2 pounds whole baby beets, trimmed and cleaned

1/4 cup olive oil

Sea salt and fresh cracked black pepper

Tian of Rainbow Chard Leaves

Tian is a French term for an oval earthenware dish used to make gratin, but it also means "quick-cooking," an apt description for these lightly seasoned pan-flashed greens. Chard is also an important nutrient for those with diabetes, as it protects the kidneys. There are several types of chard, with the stems in different colors such as white, yellow, or red. A bunch of rainbow chard contains all of the colors. This recipe is for the leaves only, so tear them from the stems, which you may want to dice, cook, and use separately.

Sauté the oil, garlic, and shallots in the oil. Once they begin to caramelize, add the chard leaves and stir constantly until the chard begins to wilt. Add the sage and season with salt and pepper to taste. Serve immediately.

Serves 4

1 tablespoon olive oil

1/2 teaspoon finely minced garlic

1/2 teaspoon finely minced shallots

3 cups rainbow chard leaves, chiffonade (about 2 pounds)

1 teaspoon julienne of fresh sage

Salt and fresh cracked black pepper

Afterlife: Dessert

The Sonoran Desert provided plenty of sweets for the native people. The prickly pear yields plump ruby-colored fruit (called *tunas* by Hispanic settlers) ready to eat fresh or boiled down to syrup, or made into sorbet or preserves. Other succulents and cacti such as the saguaro have sugary pulps eaten as a sweet by native people. Wild berries were long treasured by desert people. Fresh corn kernels were sometimes left outside in winter to freeze and made a sort of ice cream. A source of fat and protein as well as flavor, walnuts thrived. The town of Nogales, Arizona, takes its name from the Spanish word for walnut. The piñon (pinyon), or pine nut, is a signature of the Southwest.

You will find many of these flavors in the desserts made at Kai using local ingredients and traditional methods. These are a few that are not too difficult to prepare at home and that may introduce you to some new and exciting flavors.

◎◎◎◎◎◎◎◎◎◎◎◎◎◎◎◎◎◎◎◎◎◎◎

Goat's Milk Cheesecake on Mesquite Meal Crust
with Fennel-Pistachio Crumbs 94
Fry Bread with Ibarra Chocolate and Kahlúa Ice Cream
and Ancho Caramel Sauce 95
Three Sisters Crème Brûlée: Squash with Candied Pepitas,
Fire-Roasted Corn with Huitlacoche Biscotti,
Mount Pima Anise with Candied Red Bean Paste 96
Local Olives Prepared Three Ways 99

Goat's Milk Cheesecake on Mesquite Meal Crust with
Fennel-Pistachio Crumbs

Three Sisters Crème Brûlée: Squash with Candied Pepitas, Fire-Roasted Corn with Huitlacoche Biscotti, Mount Pima Anise with Candied Red Bean Paste

Here is a dessert version of the "three sisters" of corn, squash, and beans. Make all of the components ahead of time, then just before serving torch the brûlées and assemble the plates with the candied fennel and red bean sauce. This is not only delicious, it is a gorgeous presentation. It is worth buying a home kitchen brûlée torch, which costs between $20 and $30 in most kitchen stores.

Butternut Squash Crème Brûlée

2 cinnamon sticks

4 whole cloves

2 whole star anise pods

1 tablespoon ground cardamom

2 teaspoons ground ginger

½ cup maple syrup

2½ cups plus 3 tablespoons sugar (divided)

4 pounds butternut squash, peeled, seeded, and medium-diced

Water

1 quart heavy cream

8 egg yolks

1. Preheat the oven to 325 degrees.

2. In a sauté pan, toast the cinnamon, clove, star anise, cardamom, and ginger. Cool the spices and grind to a fine powder.

3. Sprinkle the toasted spices, along with the maple syrup and ½ cup plus 2 tablespoons of sugar, over the butternut squash. Put a little water in the bottom of the pan and roast the squash for about 30 to 40 minutes; poke the squash with a toothpick to check for doneness. Once cooked through, cool and puree the squash in a food processor. You should have about 2½ cups of puree.

4. Heat the cream in a saucepan. In a mixing bowl whisk the egg yolks, 1 cup plus 1 tablespoon sugar, and squash puree. Temper the eggs with the heavy cream, then combine this mixture with the egg, sugar, and squash puree. Bake in individual ceramic dishes or ramekins at 300 degrees for 15 to 20 minutes, or until a toothpick inserted in the center comes out clean.

Fire-Roasted Corn Crème Brûlée

8 ears corn on the cob

2 quarts heavy cream

1 vanilla bean

1 cup plus 2 tablespoons sugar

14 egg yolks

1. Roast the ears of corn in their husks wrapped in tin foil for 20 minutes in a 350-degree oven. Allow the corn to cool before husking and shucking.

2. Lower the oven to 300 degrees.

3. In a saucepan steep the corn kernels, heavy cream, and vanilla bean together to bring out the essence of the corn. In a mixing bowl whisk the sugar and egg yolks together. Strain the cream mixture to remove any corn kernels or skin. Use some of the strained cream mixture to temper the eggs before adding it all. Bake in individual dishes, such as ramekins, at 300 degrees for 20 to 30 minutes. Check for doneness by sticking a toothpick into the brûlée. If it comes out clean, the brûlée is done.

Mount Pima Anise Crème Brûlée

2 quarts heavy cream
1 vanilla bean
$^1/_2$ bag Pima tea (see
   Glossary)
10 ounces sugar
14 egg yolks

1. In a saucepan steep the heavy cream, vanilla bean, and tea together over low-to-medium heat to bring out the tea/vanilla bean essence. In a mixing bowl beat the sugar and egg yolks together.
2. Strain the cream mixture to remove the vanilla bean pod and tea leaves. Use some of this mixture to temper the sugar and egg mixture. Pour into small oven-proof serving dishes or ramekins. Bake at 300 degrees until set.

Candied Red Bean Paste

$^1/_2$ pound adzuki beans,
   soaked overnight
$1^1/_2$ quarts mineral water
$^2/_3$ cups sugar
$^2/_3$ cup hazelnut oil

Cook the pre-soaked beans in the mineral water over medium heat until cooked through and tender, about 30 minutes. Strain the beans and put one-fourth of them into a food processor with the sugar. Puree with the hazelnut oil. Then, in a bowl, fold in the whole beans and allow to cool.

To Serve

Candied Pepitas (page 116)
Huitlacoche Biscotti
   (page 36)
Kai Brûlée Sugar (page 115)

For each serving, arrange the three small brûlée dishes on a long, rectangular plate or a wooden board. Place some Candied Pepitas on the Butternut Squash Crème Brûlée. Set a Huitlacoche Biscotti over the dish of Fire-Roasted Corn Crème Brûlée. Garnish the Mount Pima Anise Crème Brûlée with a dollop of the Candied Red Bean Paste. Sprinkle all three with Kai Brûlée Sugar.

Serve this dessert with a Madeira, such as the five-year-old Broadbent, for a classic pairing of burnt cream and cooked wine.

Serves 6 to 8

Local Olives Prepared Three Ways

Each component of this dessert can be made and enjoyed by itself, but together, the Blue Cornmeal Scones with Candied Olives, the Olive Oil and Citrus Gelato, and the Avocado and Olive Oil Chocolate Truffles present a new way to experience this fruit. A signature dessert at Kai, it is made with locally grown olives and olive oil.

Blue Cornmeal Scones with Candied Olives

1. Preheat the oven to 350 degrees.

2. Mix the dry ingredients in a large bowl. Then add the cream, honey, and candied olives and mix the dry ingredients into a dough. Let the dough rest for 15 minutes at room temperature.

3. Roll out the dough to a 3-inch thickness and cut into desired shapes. At Kai circles replace the traditional triangles. Lay the shapes on a buttered sheet pan and sprinkle with sugar.

4. Bake for 15 minutes. Turn once and bake another 10 minutes.

Makes 24 small scones

1 cup blue cornmeal (see Shopping Guide)
1/2 cup all-purpose flour
3 tablespoons baking powder
1/4 cup sugar
1 tablespoon salt
1 cup heavy cream
1/2 cup honey
1 cup candied chopped olives (see Chef's Note)
Butter to grease pan
1/2 cup (approximate) large-grain sugar for garnish

Olive Oil and Citrus Gelato

In a food processor, combine the egg yolks and sugar on high speed until the batter reaches the ribbon stage. Keeping the speed on high, add the olive oil. Then, on low speed, add the milk and heavy cream. Add the blood orange zest and mix thoroughly. Put the mixture in an ice cream machine and freeze according to instructions.

Makes 3 quarts

12 egg yolks
1 3/4 cups sugar
1 1/2 cups extra virgin olive oil
3 quarts milk
1 quart heavy cream
Zest from 1 blood orange

Avocado and Olive Oil Chocolate Truffles

1. In a saucepan, heat the heavy cream and vanilla extract. Then add the chocolate and allow it to melt while stirring. Pour this mixture into small pyramid molds and refrigerate overnight.

2. Using an ice cream scoop, remove a ball of the chocolate from the bottom of each pyramid and fill it with 1 teaspoon of olive oil and 1 teaspoon of avocado oil. Melt the scooped out chocolate so it is pliable and use it to cover and seal the hole. Refrigerate overnight or until the oil sets.

Makes about 2 dozen truffles

1 quart heavy cream
2 teaspoons vanilla extract
2 pounds 58 percent chocolate
1/2 pound 65 percent chocolate
1/2 cup (approximate) olive oil
1/2 cup (approximate) avocado oil

Gooseberry and Wild Berry
Compote (page 113)
Sprigs of edible lavender

To Serve

At Kai this is served on a rectangular piece of wood, but you can use a long plate. First scatter some olives along the dish or board, then space each of the three components on the dish. On the left spoon out a pool of Gooseberry and Wild Berry Compote and top it with a Blue Corn Scone and a sprig of lavender. Put a scoop of Olive Oil and Citrus Gelato in the center and a truffle on the other side.

Pair this dessert with Torbreck "Bothie," a light-colored mellow wine. The sweetness isn't overbearing, and helps highlight the olive flavor and cleanse the palate between the three different olive variations.

ⓞⓞⓞⓞⓞⓞⓞⓞⓞⓞⓞⓞⓞⓞ
Chef O'Dowd Notes: If you cannot find prepared candied olives, simply slice up some green (or black) olives, toss them in sugar, and lay them out on a board or sheet pan for about an hour.
ⓞⓞⓞⓞⓞⓞⓞⓞⓞⓞⓞⓞⓞⓞ

Finishing Touches

Flavored vinegars and oils, salad dressings, rubs, sauces, and garnishes can be used in a variety of recipes in this book as well as in your own recipes. There are also several finishing salts that add just the right touch to a steak or other dish.

◉◉◉◉◉◉◉◉◉◉◉◉◉◉◉◉◉◉◉◉◉◉◉

Flavored Vinegars and Oils

Flavored vinegars are widely available in fine food markets and online, but they are a bit pricey. If you are so inclined, you could make them at home. Herbal vinegars are easy: Simply put a few sprigs of fresh tarragon or other favorite herb into a quart of vinegar and let it sit for a week or so. Begin with basic white distilled vinegar, or white wine or rice wine.

For Basic Herbal Vinegar

First, sterilize some Mason jars or other glass containers in which you can seal and store the vinegar. Be sure there are no cracks and that cork or metal tops fit snugly. Wash and simmer the jars in hot water for about 10 minutes, then turn them upside down on a towel to drain. Do this just before you make the vinegar, so the jars are warm when you begin.

Use the freshest herbs, and be sure there are no bruises on them. Begin with one kind of herb until you get used to it; then combine any number of flavors. Wash sprigs of herbs and put them about ⅓ of the way up in a jar, bruising them a bit in the process to release flavor. Heat the vinegar on the stove just to the boiling point and pour it over the herbs, filling the jar about ½ full. Allow to cool and close the jar with the lid or cork.

Store the herbal vinegar in the refrigerator for a week or two. Shake the jars gently every 3 or 4 days to help meld the flavors. When ready, strain the vinegar through a fine sieve lined with a coffee filter. This preserves the life of the vinegar.

For Basic Lavender Vinegar

2 cups vinegar (white or wine)

2 tablespoons dried or fresh edible lavender buds

In a stainless steel pan, bring the vinegar and lavender to a boil. Remove it from the heat and allow it to cool for 15 minutes before straining into a sterile jar. Store as above.

VARIATIONS

For lavender berry vinegar add ½ cup fresh berries along with the lavender and vinegar and proceed as above.

For lavender saguaro vinegar, add some saguaro syrup to the vinegar before using.

Fennel Oil

Flavored and colored oils are used for garnishing dishes. This one makes a bright green oil that garnishes the Lion's Paw Baja Scallops and Poached Salsify (page 44).

Toast the fennel seeds in a sauté pan and cool. In a blender, puree the toasted fennel seeds, fennel fronds, and spinach. Add the oil until blended. Using a coffee filter and fine sieve, strain the oil. Pour the oil into a squeezable bottle to use to drizzle around scallops or other dishes.

Makes 2 cups

/4 cup fennel seeds

¯ cup fennel fronds

1 cups spinach, cleaned

2 cups olive oil

Vinaigrettes and Marinades

Blood Orange Vinaigrette

At Kai, this vinaigrette is used with hand-picked lettuces from the children at Gila Crossing School, but you can use it on most green salads. Blood oranges have a very particular tart sweetness, so don't substitute a regular orange for this recipe. Chipotle is a dried and smoked jalapeño with a smoky flavor and a hint of chocolate. Use the dressing sparingly so it doesn't overpower the baby greens, and dress the salad just before serving. This recipe makes more than enough for six salads, but you can keep the leftover dressing in the fridge for a day or two.

Place the fresh-squeezed juices, vinegar, chipotle, and honey in a blender. Blend on low speed and slowly drizzle in the canola oil until the dressing emulsifies. Finish with salt and pepper to taste.

Makes 2 cups

6 blood oranges, juiced

1½ Gila River or other ruby red grapefruit, juiced

½ cup rice wine vinegar

1 reconstituted chipotle, seeded and chopped

¼ cup Happy Bear honey (see Shopping Guide)

½ cup Queen Creek or other canola oil

Sea salt and fresh cracked black pepper to taste

Chef Strong Notes: The flavors of this dressing are potent but subtle, and we don't want to overpower them by using olive oil. Canola oil is more like a blank canvas that doesn't lend its own personality to the mix.

Saguaro-Lavender Vinaigrette

1 teaspoon dried edible
  lavender

6 teaspoons saguaro syrup
  (see Shopping Guide)

1/2 cup port wine

1 small shallot, chopped

1/2 cup berry vinegar, such
  as raspberry or blueberry

1 1/2 cups Queen Creek or
  other canola oil

Sea salt and pepper

Saguaro syrup is a thick, mahogany-colored, sweet, smoky essence that is second to none on the planet. The seeds of the saguaro (a sacred plant here) are hand-harvested from the fruit and slowly roasted over mesquite. The resulting syrup is extremely expensive and hard to get. At Kai it is combined with edible lavender, which has a slight mint flavor, and used to dress hand-picked baby lettuces.

In a small saucepan reduce the lavender, saguaro syrup, and port by half over medium heat. Strain this mixture and put into a blender. Add the shallot and vinegar and puree while slowly adding the oil until it emulsifies. Add salt and pepper to taste.

Makes 2 cups

Golden Tomato Vinaigrette

1 1/2 teaspoons Queen
  Creek or other canola oil
  (approximate)

1/2 papaya, peeled, seeded,
  and chopped

1/2 mango, peeled, seeded,
  and chopped

2 golden tomatoes,
  chopped

1/2 yellow bell pepper,
  seeded and chopped

1 cloves garlic, minced

1/2 shallot, minced

1/4 cup white wine

1 cup chicken stock

1 1/2 teaspoons white
  vinegar

Salt and pepper to taste

In a sauté pan with the oil, sweat all the fruit and vegetables until soft. Deglaze the pan with the white wine and reduce by half. Add the chicken stock and reduce the heat to a simmer. Cook until all the vegetables are tender, about 15 minutes. Puree in a blender. Add the vinegar and adjust the seasoning with salt and pepper. Strain in a fine sieve and allow to cool before using.

Makes 1 cup

Chile Jam Marinade

In saucepan simmer all ingredients for about 15 minutes. Cool and use as a marinade with fish.

Makes 1 cup

2 jars of New Mexico Chile Jam (Native Seeds/ SEARCH)
1/2 cup soy milk
3 tablespoons dark molasses
5 tablespoons l'itoi onions cut on bias (or scallions)

Pima Citrus-Vanilla Juice Marinade

Mix all ingredients together in a large bowl and marinate overnight to infuse the citrus and vanilla.

Makes about 1 1/2 cups

Zest of 1 orange
Zest of 1 lemon
Zest of 3 limes
Juice of 3 oranges
Juice of 3 limes
Juice of 1 lemon
1 vanilla bean, cleaned
1/2 cup rice vinegar
1/2 tablespoon chipotle puree

General Herb Marinade

This is a terrific marinade for meat, and at Kai it is made fresh daily and used for buffalo and elk. The ingredients are simply fresh oregano, basil, garlic, and olive oil with salt and pepper added to taste. If you use it at once, roast the garlic first so that most of the flavor is extracted. If you plan to make it ahead and store for future use, use raw garlic and heat everything in the oil to infuse the flavor. Store the marinade in the refrigerator when it cools.

Fresh herbs are often sold in bunches—several twigs bound at the stem— or in plastic packets in supermarkets and gourmet stores. The amounts here are very general, but try for equal amounts of oregano and basil and increase the amount of garlic and oil proportionately.

Combine the herbs, garlic, and seasonings with enough oil to make a paste to rub all around the meat.

For preparing a larger batch to use and store, combine the ingredients in a saucepan and bring to a boil. Then remove from the heat and allow the mixture to steep until cooled. Strain and store the marinade in the fridge.

Makes 2 to 3 cups

1 bunch fresh oregano
1 bunch fresh basil
1 roasted head of garlic (or peeled garlic cloves)
Oil to incorporate
Salt and pepper to taste

Chihuacle Negro Puree

15 Chihuacle negro chiles, seeded and toasted
1/2 cup honey
1 shallot, diced
1 cup red wine vinegar
2 oranges, juiced
2 limes, juiced

The chihuacle (chee-wah-lee) is a hard-to-find pepper from Oaxaca, Mexico. It looks a bit like a miniature bell pepper and has intense flavor. It is popular in the moles of southern Mexico.

In a saucepan combine the chiles, honey, shallot, and vinegar and simmer until reduced to a syrup consistency. Pour into a blender and add the citrus juices; puree and strain through a fine sieve.

Makes 1 cup

Piquillo Pepper Sauce

Canola oil
1 1/2 yellow onions, diced small
2 tablespoons minced garlic
2 cups piquillo peppers, grilled and chopped
2 tablespoons aged sherry vinegar
1 1/2 quarts chicken stock
2 tablespoons Santa Cruz chili powder
Sea salt and cracked black pepper to taste

1. Heat the oil in a saucepan and sweat the onions, garlic, and piquillo peppers until soft, about 7 or 8 minutes. Deglaze the pan with the sherry vinegar and reduce to near glacé. Add the chicken stock and reduce again by half.
2. Pour the mixture into a blender, add chili powder, and puree (be careful if it is still hot) and then strain it through a fine sieve. Season with salt and pepper.

Makes about 2 cups

Piquillo Pepper Chili Base for Chemaith

2 dried chipotle chiles
2 dried pasilla chiles
2 dried guajillo peppers
2 cups mineral water
1 cup port vinegar
18 piquillo peppers, grilled
1 tablespoon roasted garlic
3 tablespoons honey
Sea salt and pepper

This sauce, a bit different from the previous one, is used for the Chile Chemaith Bread on page 33.

Rehydrate the dried chiles in the water and vinegar. Add the next 3 ingredients and puree in a blender until smooth, then strain through a fine sieve. Season with salt and pepper.

Makes about 6 cups

Hibiscus Syrup

Hibiscus Syrup is available at fine food markets and online, but it is simple to make at home. Edible flowers are dried and slightly sweetened and sold at supermarkets and gourmet stores. (You may find them in the same section as dried fruit.) Copper pans are best for maintaining an even heat, so if you have one, use it for this syrup.

1 pound sugar
1 quart water
2 ounces hibiscus flowers
(see Shopping Guide)

In a copper saucepan, bring all the ingredients to a boil. Lower the heat and simmer until thickened. Puree, strain, and cool.

Makes 2 cups

Ancho Chile-Caramel Sauce

This spicy sweet sauce is served with the Ice Cream and Fry Bread Dessert at Kai, but it is good to have on hand for any ice cream dessert.

5 cups sugar
1/2 cup water
1/2 ancho chile, seeded
1/8 cup light corn syrup
1 1/2 quarts heavy cream
2 ounces butter (1/2 stick)

Put the sugar into a copper saucepan with the water, ancho, and corn syrup. Bring to a boil and simmer until amber colored. Add the heavy cream and finish with butter. Strain out the chile and allow the sauce to cool. This will keep in the refrigerator for several days.

Makes about 2 cups

2 tablespoons barbecue
  spice
2 tablespoons Mexican
  cumin
2 tablespoons Spanish
  paprika
2 tablespoons Jamaican jerk
  seasoning
2 tablespoons granulated
  garlic
2 tablespoons garlic powder
2 tablespoons fresh ground
  cinnamon
2 tablespoons Chinese five-
  spice powder
2 tablespoons chili powder
4 tablespoons kosher salt
2 cups cocoa powder
2 tablespoons chipotle
  powder
2 tablespoons Guajillo
  powder
2 tablespoons chili powder

Dust and Mud

Mole Dust
This rub is used on meat dishes at Kai. You can make a batch and keep it on hand. One ingredient is barbecue spice, which is a well-guarded secret at Kai, so you may have to substitute one of your own.

Mix all the ingredients together and store in a sealed container in a cool dry place.

Makes about 2$\frac{1}{2}$ cups

$\frac{1}{4}$ cup dried mango powder
$\frac{1}{3}$ cup curry powder
$\frac{1}{4}$ cup Jamaican jerk
  seasoning
$\frac{1}{3}$ cup tandoori powder
$\frac{1}{2}$ cup sandalwood powder
  (see Shopping Guide)

Dried Mango and Sandalwood Dust
Mix all the ingredients together and store in a dry container.

Makes about 1$\frac{2}{3}$ cups

Tomatillo Mud

Grill the husked tomatillos for 5 or 10 minutes until soft. Sauté the onion, poblano pepper, jalapeño, and garlic. Add the grilled tomatillos and chicken stock. Bring to a boil, lower the heat, and simmer for about 15 minutes to allow the flavors to combine. Puree in a blender with cilantro, add the crema and lime juice, and season with salt and pepper. Store in the refrigerator.

Makes 2 to 3 cups

12 to 15 tomatillos, husked (peeled)
1 yellow onion, chopped
1 poblano pepper chopped
1 jalapeño pepper, chopped
4 cloves garlic
2 cups chicken stock
1 bunch cilantro
1 cup Mexican crema (see Glossary)
Fresh lime juice to taste
Sea salt and cracked black pepper

Salsas, Chutneys, and Compotes

Red and Yellow Teardrop Tomato Salsa

Lightly toss all the ingredients together and marinate in the refrigerator for at least an hour or overnight to infuse the flavors.

Makes 1 cup

$\frac{1}{2}$ cup red teardrop tomatoes, cut in half lengthwise
$\frac{1}{2}$ cup yellow teardrop tomatoes, cut in half lengthwise
2 tablespoons coarsely chopped cilantro leaves
1 tablespoon extra-virgin olive oil
1 teaspoon white balsamic vinegar

Golden Raisin Compote

1 bottle Sauterne (about 2
  cups)
2 cups golden raisins
1/2 cup mint leaves
1 cup sugar
3 tablespoons Hatch chili
  powder

Put all ingredients except the Hatch chili powder into a saucepan over low heat. Reduce to a syrupy consistency. Remove from the heat and fold in the chili powder. Cool and reserve.

Makes 2 cups

Cranberry Compote

Cheesecloth and string
1/2 bunch flowering thyme
1/2 bunch Mexican oregano
1/2 head elephant garlic
1/2 tablespoon Tasmanian
  black peppercorns
1 fresh bay leaf
1/2 tablespoon finely
  chopped shallots
1 tablespoon canola oil
2 cups fresh cranberries
3 cups mineral water
1/2 cup lavender vinegar
  (see page 102)
1 cup sugar
1 1/4 cups dried cherries
1 orange, juiced and zested

1. Make a sachet with the cheesecloth and string for the thyme, oregano, garlic, peppercorns, and bay leaf.

2. In a saucepan sweat the shallots in oil. Add the cranberries, water, vinegar, sugar, cherries, orange juice and zest, and the sachet. Allow the compote to simmer until thickened and reduced by half. Remove the sachet and let cool.

Makes about 2 cups

Rhubarb Chutney

2 tablespoons minced garlic
2 tablespoons minced
  shallots
1 tablespoon canola oil
2 1/2 pounds rhubarb stalks,
  diced small
2 tablespoons sugar
1/2 cup lavender vinegar
  (see page 102)

1. In a saucepan, sweat the garlic and shallots in oil. Then add the rhubarb, sugar, and vinegar. Cook over medium heat until it has a thick and chunky consistency.

2. Allow the chutney to cool, then store in the refrigerator.

Makes about 2 cups

Plum Chutney
This is part of the pork tenderloin dish at Kai, but it is delicious with most meats and poultry.

Simmer all the ingredients in a saucepan until thickened and reduced by half. Let cool.

Makes 2 cups

8 plums, chopped
3 apples, chopped
1½ cups orange marmalade
½ cup sugar
1⅛ cup lavender vinegar (see page 102)
¼ cup port wine

Gooseberry and Wild Berry Compote

1. Put all the ingredients, except the cornstarch slurry, into a large saucepan and cook on low heat until cooked, approximately 20 to 30 minutes. This should be thicker than an ordinary compote.
2. Add the slurry (cornstarch mixed with some water) to thicken and bind the compote. Puree briefly in a blender or with a stick blender, but the compote should be chunky. Strain out some of the liquid.

Yield: 2 to 3 cups

4 cups blackberries
2 cups gooseberries
2 cups blueberries
3 whole figs
½ can lychees
½ cup diced (small) Mexican papaya
2 tablespoons strawberry sauce or 4 whole strawberries
½ teaspoon lavender berry vinegar (see page 102)
2 tablespoons blood orange puree
⅓ cup sugar
1 tablespoon cornstarch slurry

Garnishes

There are many ways to garnish a dish, using colored oils, micro herbs and greens, and crisped pieces of vegetable or breads. If you cannot get micro herbs and greens (very tiny young plants), use the smallest leaf or sprig from the fully grown plants.

Finishing Salts

One garnish that people sometimes forget is finishing sea salts, which add a new texture or tang to the dish. For example, Maldon salt from Britain has a larger flake and adds a crunch when sprinkled lightly over warm tenderloin of beef. Here are some finishing salts that you may find interesting:

Maldon salt from Britain is like a sea spray. It has fewer additives than other salts and no bitter aftertaste. Crumble some flakes between your fingers onto the food.

Murray River salt from Australia's largest river has peach-colored flakes with a mild flavor. Crystals melt quickly and evenly. The color comes from the carotene in the algae.

Celtic sea salt from the coast of Brittany is naturally moist and rich in trace minerals. It is hand-harvested with wooden rakes so that no metal touches the salt. It is stone-ground into textures from coarse to extra fine.

Italian sea salt is from the coast of Sicily, Europe's oldest salt marsh. Lower in sodium than table salt, it has a delicate flavor that is suitable for salads, sauces, and for garnishing bruschetta. These salts from Trapani and Marsala are more famous there than the wines.

Jurassic sea salt is from Utah, where there was once a sea that left deposits of pure natural salt. The pink color comes from trace rock minerals caught in the deposits. It is slightly bitter.

Hawaiian red sea salt is traditional table salt in Hawaii and also used to preserve foods. Volcanic baked red clay gives it the pink color. It is excellent with beef and pork and available in fine and coarse grains. Black salt is also available from Hawaii.

Flor de Sel from Portugal is an artisan sea salt made of young crystals that form on the surface of salt ponds in the coastal wetlands of the Algarve. It is mellow with a light crunch and slightly sweet, delicate flavor.

Smoked sea salt from Maine is naturally smoked over wood—alder, apple, hickory, or mesquite—to infuse the wood flavor into the salt. Smoked sea salt adds flavor to soups, sandwiches, salads. It is perfect for grilling and roasting, especially salmon.

Korean sea salt is light gray and irregular in size. It has a coarse texture and robust flavor that make it ideal for cabbage dishes.

Japanese sea salt is less "salty" than some others and has a taste of seaweed.

Kai Brûlée Sugar

Like salt, sugar comes in a variety of textures, colors, and depth of sweetness. Large-crystal sugars and colored sugars are widely available in bakery sections of most supermarkets and gourmet stores. Here is a finishing sugar that is made at Kai to top the crème brûlée. This calls for a pound of each type of sugar, but you can make less.

1 pound white sugar
1 pound brown sugar

Mix the sugars together and spread them onto a sheet pan. Bake at 350 degrees for about an hour, stirring the sugar every 20 minutes. Cool the sugar and let it harden on the pan. Then break it up and grind it into a fine powder.

Lavender Tuilles

Tuille is a French word for a special cookie that is placed over a mold when it is hot from the oven to form a "tile." At Kai these are made with lavender and are a pretty and crispy garnish for foie gras brûlée. Lavender is from the mint family. This herb has spiky flowers and a wonderful fragrance. But be subtle with it; too much can be overwhelming.

1 pound flour
1 pound powdered sugar
1 pound butter at room temperature
9 egg whites
1 teaspoon dried lavender

Mix all the ingredients with the paddle attachment of your mixer. Form the dough into small rounds about ¼ inch high and 4 inches in diameter. Bake on a greased sheet pan, or use a Silpat liner for the pan, for 6 minutes at 300 degrees. Quickly lift the rounds from the pan with a spatula and form into desired shapes. For example, if you want a bowl shape, lay the tuille over the end of a glass until it hardens into the shape.

Makes about 2 dozen

Candied Pepitas

1 egg white

½ pound pepitas (pumpkin seeds), about 1 cup

1 teaspoon ground cinnamon

1 teaspoon ground ginger

½ teaspoon cloves ground

2 tablespoons sugar

Preheat the oven to 300 degrees. Beat the egg whites in a bowl until frothy. Add the pepitas, spices, and sugar, and mix thoroughly so that the egg white coats all the seeds. Spread them onto a sheet pan and bake for about 6 minutes. Store them in a cool place until ready to use.

Makes 1 cup

Candied Fennel

1 cup sugar

1 cup water

1 fennel bulb, cleaned and sliced thin

In a copper saucepan over medium heat, make a simple syrup with the sugar and water. Bring to a boil and dip the sliced fennel into the syrup and place the slices gently on a Silpat-lined sheet pan. Bake at 300 degrees for 30 minutes. Turn and bake for another 30 minutes.

Mushroom Mix for Garnish

⅓ cup brown clamshell mushrooms

⅓ cup white clamshell mushrooms

⅓ cup seasonal mushrooms

2 tablespoons canola oil (approximate)

Several sprigs of fresh thyme

2 garlic cloves, peeled and crushed

Salt and pepper

Clean and slice the mushrooms. Heat the oil in a sauté pan and add the mushrooms, fresh thyme, and garlic and cook until caramelized. Season with salt and pepper and cool until ready to use.

Makes about 1 cup

GLOSSARY OF NATIVE AMERICAN AND DESERT FOODS

Names in parentheses indicate source information, which can be found in the Shopping Guide.

Aji amarillo. A rich golden-colored chili powder made from the yellow aji chile, aji amarillo has a hot, fruity flavor and is used in salsas, ceviches, sauces, or pickles. (Native Seeds/SEARCH)

Amaranth. A tall plant with very broad leaves, amaranth is related to pigweed, spinach, and beets. It produces both greens and thousands of tiny edible seeds that are high in protein and calcium. Amaranth flour has a pleasant, nutty taste and makes excellent breads and pastas, and is also used in sauces. Puffed amaranth is widely available as a cereal.

Beans. One of the "three sisters," beans are large plant seeds used extensively in Native American cooking along with squash and corn. Beans can be served refried, simmered, or boiled, and varieties include the often-used pinto, black, and lima beans. Favorites at Kai include the scarlet runner and Rio Zape beans (see below).

Blue corn. Grown by the native people of the southwest for centuries, blue corn is believed to provide strength; it is often given to sick people for that reason. Traditional Hopi bread, piki, is made of blue cornmeal, sage, ashes, and water. When blue corn is ground into cornmeal it has a gray-blue color and when water is added it appears lavender. In addition to bread, blue cornmeal is used to make pancakes, soups and cereals.

Buffalo (American bison). Buffalo meat is similar to beef but with a sweeter flavor, darker color, and lower cholesterol content.

Cassava (yucca). This root plant with a tough brown skin grows in South America, Mexico, and Africa. Inside is a crisp, white flesh. There are two varieties of cassava sweet and bitter. The latter must be cooked before it can be eaten.

Chaparral. From the creosote plant that grows in the desert, chaparral was a medicinal cure-all used by the Pima and other Indians of the desert Southwest. It is also known as **Pima tea.**

Chayote. A member of the squash family, chayote resembles a light green Bartlett pear with large wrinkles. The flavor is like a combination between a cucumber and a zucchini squash. It adds texture and crunch to salads.

Chia seeds. A high-protein seed with many vitamins and antioxidants, chia used to be called "running food" because it was so energizing. According to lore, Apache warriors would tie a bag of chia seeds to their belts to sustain them on the warpath. Aztecs also used the seeds as legal tender. They are very high in omega-3. When chia seeds are mixed with water, a gel forms, and this lowers cholesterol and stabilizes blood sugar. Chia is sometimes called the "Jello of the desert."

Chihuacle chile. From Oaxaca, this chile is often hard to find. It looks like a mini-bell pepper but has intense flavor.

Chiles. Found in many types of cuisine, there are more than 200 different varieties of chile peppers. The two ways to classify chiles are by their level of heat and whether they are fresh or dry. To reduce the heat in a dish, the seeds and ribs of the chile can be removed.

Chili. Powder made from dried chiles, chili is also the name of a spicy dish made of meat and beans.

Chiltepins. These are small, wild chiles that grow in the desert.

Chimayo. A flavorful medium-hot chile that originated in the New Mexico village of Chimayo in the seventeenth century when Spanish farmers settled there, the Chimayo chile acquired legendary status and by 1900 was famous throughout the world. (Native Seeds/SEARCH)

Chimichangas. These spicy, deep-fried tortilla packets are filled with shredded (and sometimes dried) meat, cheese, rice, and/or refried beans. Once filled, the burrito edges are sealed, and the packet is deep fried. It is often garnished with salsa, guacamole, shredded cheese or sour cream—or all of the above.

Chipotle. A dried and smoked jalapeño, the chipotle pepper has a smoky flavor and a hint of chocolate. A **chipotle morita** has even more smoke.

Cholla buds (ciolim, choya). Picked from the buckthorn cholla cactus in early spring, these highly unusual buds are high in calcium. One tablespoon of buds has as much calcium as an eight-ounce glass of milk. They have blood sugar–lowering properties and are extremely low on the glycemic index. Flavor tones range from asparagus to artichoke. (Native Seeds/SEARCH and TOCA)

Chemaith. A Native American bread that is baked or grilled, Chemaith is similar to pita bread.

Cabrales. Cheese from Spain.

Corn. A plant indigenous to North America, corn is considered sacred by many Native Americans. Dried corn is used to make cornmeal and hominy (posole), and fresh corn is often mixed into salsas and salads. Along with beans and squash, corn is one of the components of the "three sisters" of agriculture.

Elk. Natives used this meat for centuries. It is also still used in chili. At Kai, the elk is from the mountains of Colorado. Like buffalo, elk meat is leaner and lower in cholesterol than beef.

Fry bread. Created from the white flour and lard that the United States Army supplied to displaced Native Americans along with canned goods, fry bread is still made by Native Americans but with many variations in texture and size. Navajos make tacos with fry bread. At Kai this bread is made with a soft interior and a slightly crispy exterior.

Guajillo chile. This chile has a shiny, smooth skin and deep, burnished red color. It is very tough and must be soaked longer than most dried chiles. (Native Seeds/SEARCH)

Happy Bear mesquite honey. Made by bees from the nectar of local mesquite tree flowers, this light-colored honey, unfiltered and unheated, comes from Saguaro Honey Farm of Tucson.

Hominy (see Posole)

Huitlacoche (cuitlacoche). This is a fungus known as "corn smut" that damages maize and sweet corn. However, it is considered a delicacy in Mexico and is preserved and sold for a higher price than corn. Ancient Aztecs purposely inoculated corn with the spores to produce this prized delicacy with a flavor that has been described as inky and mushroomy. It is widely available canned in Mexican and gourmet markets.

L'itoi onion. Similar to a scallion but with far more flavor, this rich and spicy onion is grown at Gila Crossing School.

Mesquite bean syrup and molasses. These are made by extracting the juice from the mesquite bean pods that grow abundantly in Southwestern desert.

Mesquite meal. Milled from the sun-ripened seed pod of the mesquite tree, this aromatic, high-protein, high-fiber meal can be used as a rub for meats or sprinkled on a wide variety of foods as a unique flavor enhancer. When it is used as flour, substitute mesquite meal for about one-third of the flour in your favorite recipes. It is 100 percent natural.

Mesquite tree. A hardwood tree which grows wild throughout the Southwest and northern Mexico, mesquite wood is used primarily for barbecuing and smoking foods. The wood gives off a slightly smoky, sweet flavor.

Mexican crema. The Mexican verison of crème fraîche is available in Mexican markets.

Meyer lemon. Originally from China and thought to be a cross between a true lemon and a mandarin orange, this citrus fruit was introduced to the United States in 1908. Meyer lemons are sweeter and less acidic than common lemons and have a fragrant edible skin. The trees are smaller than regular lemon trees; the fruit is yellow and rounder than a true lemon, with a slight orange tint when ripe. Meyer lemons are grown at Gila River Farms.

Mojo rojo. Originating in the Canary Islands, this spicy sauce is usually made with garlic, chili powder, cumin, and paprika, as well as vinegar and citrus. It means "red sauce."

Mole. An Aztec word meaning "mixture," this complex sauce contains many kinds of chiles and other seasonings along with chocolate. (Native Seeds/SEARCH)

Nopales. These are fresh pads of the prickly pear cactus that appear in spring and fall. *Nopales* means "cactus" in Spanish, but they were eaten as a vegetable long before the Spanish arrived on the scene. Nopales can be grilled to add flavor and diced to use in salad and salsa. When cut up or pickled, they are called **nopalitas**.

Ojo de Cabra. Its name meaning "eye of the goat," this light brown bean is a favorite in Baja, Mexico. It remains firm and richly colored after cooking with a smooth texture and sweet flavor.

Pasilla. This is a dried blackish-brown chile that is also known as *little raisin* or *chile negro*. In fresh form it is called the *chilaca*. It is mild to medium hot with a rich flavor that makes it ideal for use in sauces. You can buy it whole and powdered.

Pepicha. This Mexican herb tastes like cilantro and mint.

Pepitas. Dark green–hulled pumpkin seeds, pepitas taste delicious toasted and salted and eaten as a snack. They can also be ground and used in moles and sauces.

Pima tea (see Chaparral)

Piquillo (pequillo). The name means "little beak" because this chile pepper is long and pointed like a bird's beak. Originating in northern Spain, the piquillo is traditionally hand-picked and roasted over open fires. Then the peppers are peeled (all by hand) and packed in jars or tins. The rich, spicy sweet flavor is from the roasting.

Planking. This cooking technique, derived from Native Americans in the Northwest, imparts the flavors of the wood into the meat or fish being cooked.

Plantago seeds (psyllium). Primarily used as an astringent or antitoxin in herbal remedies for insect bites and rashes, plantago seeds also absorb water and are sometimes used in certain drinks.

Pomegranate. From red to pink-blushed yellow, pomegranate fruit contains hundreds of seeds packed in compartments that are separated by bitter, cream-colored membranes. Each tiny, edible seed is surrounded by a translucent, brilliant red pulp that has a sparkling sweet tart flavor. Pomegranates are grown throughout Asia and the Mediterranean, and at the Gila Crossing School.

Posole. Also known as **hominy,** these are dried corn kernels treated with lime to remove the hulls. Posole is a thick, hearty soup usually eaten as a main course. At Kai posole is mixed with the succotash to make a succotash/posole hash.

Prickly pear fruit. These purplish red, pear-shaped fruit of the prickly pear cactus are peeled and eaten like kiwi fruits or pureed and used in drinks, sauces, and syrups. (Pads of the prickly pear cactus are called **nopales.**)

Prickly pear pads (see Nopales)

Pueblo Hatch chiles. From the chile capital of the world, Hatch, New Mexico, these are flavorful and bright red with a good heat level.

Quinoa. Pronounced "keen-wah," this gluten-free grain is native to the Andes Mountains of Bolivia, Chile, and Peru. It is closely related to amaranth. Called "vegetable caviar" or "Inca rice," it was eaten for 5,000 years by the people of those countries. In the Inca language it means "mother grain." It makes excellent grain salads and can also be used as a thickening agent.

Rio Zape beans. A rich, dense purple heirloom bean with black lines that cooks to a lovely purple color, the Rio Zape was unearthed in the ruins of the Anasazi cliff dwelling people in the Southwest. The bean is also known as the Hopi string bean. It has a creamy texture and a complex flavor with a hint of chocolate. (Native Seeds/SEARCH)

Saguaro blossom syrup *(Bahidaj Sitol)*. This thick, mahogany-colored molasses is the rarest of the world's fruit syrups. Made from hand-harvested saguaro fruit, cooked slowly over mesquite fires, it has an unusual and deep flavor that is indescribable. (Native Seeds/SEARCH)

Saguaro seeds *(Bahidai kaij)*. Painstakingly separated from the dried saguaro fruit, these tiny black seeds are full of healthful oils and high in fiber. Roasted, they can substitute for poppyseeds (TOCA).

Scarlet runner beans. These large, purple beans with black flecks have a creamy texture and remarkable flavor. (Native Seeds/SEARCH)

Squab. Also called prairie squab, this is a young domesticated pigeon that has never flown; therefore its meat is very tender.

Squash blossoms. The flowers of squash plants were used by Native Americans for centuries and most often dipped in batter and sautéed or fried. Or, they can be used whole or cut into strips as a garnish for soups, salads, and main dishes. They are grown at the Gila Crossing School.

Sun chokes. These plants and their light-colored tubers are also known as **Jerusalem artichokes,** although the plant has no relation to Jerusalem and it is not a type of artichoke.

Another name for them is **sun roots,** which is closer to the original Native American name for the plant, a type of sunflower. Sun chokes are mild-flavored and crisp when raw. When sliced and fried they are similar to potatoes.

Tepary beans. A traditional source of protein for the desert natives, this nutty-tasting bean is highly nutritious and grows wild in the Sonoran Desert. It comes in several colors and varieties, and is delicious in salads, dips, or stews. (Native Seeds/SEARCH)

Tomatillo. A Mexican green tomato covered in a husk, the tomatillo tastes a bit like apple, lemon, and herbs.

Yucca (see Cassava).

SHOPPING GUIDE FOR NATIVE AMERICAN HERITAGE AND SPECIALTY FOODS

HERITAGE FOODS and SEEDS

Native Seeds/SEARCH (NS/S)

Online ordering: www.nativeseeds.org
Retail store:
526 North 4th Avenue
Tucson, Arizona 85705
520-622-5561

This nonprofit organization based in Tucson preserves heritage seeds and operates seed banks as well as an online shop where you can order: beans, chili powder, whole chiles, smoked chiles, mole powder, salsas and sauces, corn products, sweets, baking mixes, herbs and teas, and other goodies.

Many of the items used in the recipes in this book are available from NS/S. The organization also sponsors many food-related events such as Mole Madness, cooking classes with board member and restaurant owner Chef Janos Wilder of Tucson, book signings, photo and art exhibits, and a harvest festival. SEARCH is an acronym for Southwestern Endangered Arid Regional Clearing House.

Queen Creek Olive Mill

25062 South Meridian Road
Queen Creek, Arizona 85242
480-888-9290
www.queencreekolivemill.com
Open daily

This is a shop and restaurant as well as a mill where local olives are processed into oil. Queen Creek carries a line of olive oils, tapenade, and dressings.

Heritage Foods, USA

2370 East Stadium Boulevard, Suite 007
Ann Arbor, Michigan 48104
212-980-6603
www.heritagefoodsusa.com

Heritage Foods sells Tohono O'odham products, including white and brown tepary beans, cholla buds, saguaro syrup, saguaro seeds, corn flour, hominy, wild Guajillo honey, and jellies.

Cheri's Desert Harvest
1840 East Winsett
Tucson, Arizona 85719
800-743-1141
www.cherisdesertharvest.com

Products from the Sonoran Desert include prickly pear jellies, syrups, candies, mesquite bean syrup, and bread mixes.

Crooked Sky Farms
Frank Martin
P.O.Box 157
Glendale, Arizona 85311-0157
623-206-4435
E-mail: farmerfrank@crookedskyfarms.com

Maya's Farm
Maya Dailey
6106 South 32nd Street
Phoenix, Arizona 85042
480-236-7097
E-mail: vayaconmaya@cox.net

Conscientiously grown vegetables and herbs

One Windmill Farm
John Scott
602-738-0189
www.onewindmillfarm.com

Found at various Arizona farmers markets

Seacat Gardens
Carl Seacat
Downtown Phoenix Public Market
721 North Central Avenue
www.downtownphoenixpublicmarket.com
623-846-4624
E-mail: carl@seacat.com

Vegetables from heirloom seed stock

McClendon's Select
Bob McClendon
15888 North 77th Avenue
Peoria, Arizona 85382-3881
1-866-979-5279
www.selectcitrus.com

Citrus fruits, dates, and honey

Sonoran Date Palms
Shephard Neeley
HC-1 Box 35W
Dateland, Arizona 85333
602-738-9832
www.sonorandatepalms.com

E-mail: shephardneeley@yahoo.com

Fistiki Farms Pistachios
1797 North Cochises Stronghold Road
Cochise, Arizona 85606
1-800-442-4207

The Green Valley Pecan Company
1625 East Sahuarita Road
Sahuarita, Arizona 85629
520-791-2062
www.greenvalleypecan.com

EGGS, MEAT, and GAME

Two Wash Ranch
Dave the Egg Man
Downtown Phoenix Public Market
721 North Central Avenue
623-465-1563

Doublecheck Ranch Beef
4965 North Camino Rio
Winkelman, Arizona 85292
520-357-6515
www.doublecheckranch.com

Karen's Cimarron Ranch Natural Meats
Karen Riggs
HCR 2 Box 7152
Wilcox, Arizona 85643
520-824-3472
www.greatbeef.com
E-mail: Cimarron@vtc.net

Grass fed beef and pastured chicken

OTHER SOURCES FOR MEAT and GAME
Buffalo and venison meat, as well as wild boar bacon, are widely available in gourmet stores and also many online sources. Here are some online sources for grass-fed, free-range meat.

Snake River Farms
1555 Shoreline Drive
Boise, Idaho 83702
www.snakeriverfarms.com

Snake River Farms produces American Kobe beef and Korobuta pork that is widely available in better supermarkets and gourmet stores across the country. You can also order online.

D'Artagnan
280 Wilson Avenue
Newark, New Jersey 07105
1-800-DARTAGNAN
www.dartagnan.com

Specializes in fresh and frozen free-range and grass-fed meat and game.

The Buffalo Guys
Box 74
Elk Mountain, Wyoming 82324
888-330-8686
www.thebuffaloguys.com

Cowboy Free Range Meat
P.O. Box 1618
Jackson Hole, Wyoming 83001
1-866-435-5411
www.cowboyfreerangemeat.com

Venison America
494-B County Road A
Hudson, Wisconsin 54016
800-310-2360
E-mail: venisonamerica@aol.com

WHERE TO LEARN MORE ABOUT THE NATIVE CULTURE OF THE SONORAN DESERT

The Heard Museum
2301 North Central Avenue
Phoenix, Arizona 85004
www.heard.org

The Heard Museum provides an excellent introduction to the history, culture, and art of the Southwest native peoples. This museum is world famous for its extensive American Indian collections, unique exhibits, special events, and educational programming. The museum was founded in 1929 by Dwight B. and Maie Bartlett Heard, a prominent Phoenix couple who moved there in 1895 from Chicago. They opened the museum so they could share their collection of American Indian artifacts and art. The museum has recently expanded with branches in Scottsdale and also in Surprise, Arizona.

The collections include many artifacts related to agriculture and food preparation of the local Pima and Maricopa tribes, such as baskets lined with pitch to make them waterproof, as well as baskets used for serving and carrying. (Small models of these baskets are now made for tourists.) You might see a fruit picking stick or a water jug resting in the fork of a tree branch.

The Gila Crossing School children maintain an exhibition garden at the museum, sponsored by the Thunderbirds, a charitable group that works with the Education Department. During the Indian Market in March, children give demonstrations about their garden here.

With library and archives, the museum is a valuable resource of information. The shop is one of the best for books and art on native cultures. The education center includes classrooms for school tours and workshops. Nearly 400 schools in 20 states use the museum as a curriculum source.

More than half the visitors come from states other than Arizona, and about eight percent are international visitors.

Pueblo Grande Museum and Archeological Park
4619 East Washington Street
Phoenix, Arizona 85034
602-495-0901
www.phoenix.gov/PARKS/pueblo

This is an archeological site, museum, and repository to collect, preserve and interpret cultural materials from the site of the Pueblo Grande and the greater Southwest. Part of the City of Phoenix Parks and Recreation Department since 1929, it includes the ruins of a 1,500-year-old Hohokam village, an 800-year-old platform mound, ball court, and prehistoric houses. The archaeological park includes some of the last remaining intact Hohokam irrigation canals. There are also changing exhibitions, guided tours, public archaeology programs, and a shop.

Huhugam Heritage Center

Gila River Indian Community
4759 North Maricopa Road
Chandler, Arizona 85226
520-796-3500
www.huhugam.com

This is the Gila River Indian Community's new endeavor and includes the antique baskets created by the Akimel O'Odham, who, with the Pee Posh people, form the community. The heritage center's architecture was designed to resemble Sivan Vah Ki, better known as Casa Grande Ruins National Monument, about forty-five minutes' drive away (see below). The site's four-story central structure was part of a Hohokam complex built in the 1200s or 1300s.

Casa Grande Ruins National Monument

1100 West Ruins Drive
Coolidge, Arizona 85228
520-723-3172
www.nps.gov/cagr/

Operated by the National Park Service, Casa Grande allows you to explore the wonder and mystery of the ancient Hohokam. The Big House of the Casa Grande Ruins is one of the largest prehistoric structures ever built in North America. Its purpose remains as much a mystery as the people who built it, but there is evidence of wide-scale irrigation farming and trade. It is still used for ceremonies by the tribal people.

Akimel O'otham legend says that the large structure at Casa Grande (Sivan Vahki), constructed about seven centuries ago, was built by the son of a beautiful woman who dwelt in the nearby mountains. She was so fair that all the handsome men came to court her and pay tribute with gifts of food. They came in vain, however, for she would marry none of them. From the stores of food gifts, however, she was able to feed all of the people in times of famine. Once, as she lay sleeping, a drop of rain fell upon her navel and she became pregnant. She gave birth to a son, Sivano, or Morning Green, who was the builder of all these houses. Here he governed a large empire, long before the Spanish came.

Desert Botanical Garden

1201 North Galvin Parkway
Phoenix, Arizona 85008
480-941-1225.
www.dbg.org.

Botanical exhibits, gardening classes, plant sales, and so on.

Arizona–Sonoran Desert Museum

202 North Kinney Road
Tucson, Arizona 85743
520-883-2702
www.desertmuseum.org.

The museum's mission is to inspire people to live in harmony with the natural world by fostering love, appreciation, and understanding of the Sonoran Desert. Many programs help you learn about the plants and wildlife of the desert.

Tucson Botanical Gardens

2150 North Alveron Way

Tucson, Arizona 85712

www.tucsonbotanical.org

Programs celebrate the desert plants.

Tohono Chul Park

7366 North Paseo del Norte

Tucson, Arizona 85704

520-742-6455.

www.tohonochulpark.org

A park that celebrates the desert in art, music, and guided tours.

Tohono O'odham Community Action (TOCA)

www.tocaonline.org

This grassroots organization on the Tohono O'odham Reservation seeks to return the native people to the healthful diets of their past and reduce the rate of diabetes. It does this through producing, processing, and distributing food along with education and culture.

The National Museum of the American Indian (NMAI)

www.nmai.si.edu

There are several branches of this museum operated by The Smithsonian Institution in Washington, D.C.; New York; and Maryland, plus several resource centers.

NMAI on the National Mall

Fourth Street and Independence Avenue, S.W.

Washington, D.C. 20560

202-633-1000

The Mitsitam Café at this branch serves Native American cuisine. The word *mitsitam*, in the language of the Delaware and Piscataway peoples, means "let's eat." Visitors can enhance their museum experience by sampling indigenous foods. The cafe features native foods from the western hemisphere, including the Southwest, Northwest Coast, Mesoamerica, and the Great Plains. Each food station depicts regional life ways related to cooking techniques, ingredients, and flavors found in traditional and contemporary dishes.

NMAI in New York

The George Gustav Heye Center

Alexander Hamilton U.S. Custom House

One Bowling Green

New York, New York 10004

212-514-3700

NMAI in Maryland

Cultural Resources Center

4220 Silver Hill Road

Suitland, Maryland 20746

301-238-1435

Ira Hayes Memorials

Ira Hayes, one of the most famous Pima Indians, was the reluctant hero of Iwo Jima who was immortalized in Johnny Cash's rendition of "The Ballad of Ira Hayes." While he is forever remembered in the bronze statue in Washington, D.C., and is buried at Arlington National Cemetery, Hayes is also honored by memorials in his hometown of Sacaton and as the namesake for the Ira B. Hayes Memorial High School and library.

Born on the Gila River Indian Reservation in 1923, Hayes was the oldest of eight children of Nancy and Joe Hayes. Raised by a deeply religious mother (Presbyterian) who read the Bible aloud to her children, Ira attended elementary school in Sacaton. He had good grades and continued to do well in school but quit at nineteen to enlist in the Marines. The tribe approved and sent him off to war, where he specialized in parachute training and his buddies dubbed him Chief Falling Cloud. Ira was sent to the South Pacific, where he happened to be on Mount Suribachi as one of six men planting the U.S. flag when that famous photograph was taken. After the war Hayes was recruited with the other two survivors of that photograph to meet the president and be paraded through thirty-two cities as a hero. He was a reluctant hero and kept things inside. Back home he worked at menial jobs but also found solace in alcohol, which finally killed him in 1955. Today it might have been recognized that, like many soldiers returning from war, he was suffering from post-traumatic stress disorder.

METRIC CONVERSION TABLES

APPROXIMATE U.S. METRIC EQUIVALENTS

Liquid Ingredients

U.S. MEASURES	METRIC	U.S. MEASURES	METRIC
1/4 TSP.	1.23 ML	2 TBSP.	29.57 ML
1/2 TSP.	2.36 ML	3 TBSP.	44.36 ML
3/4 TSP.	3.70 ML	1/4 CUP	59.15 ML
1 TSP.	4.93 ML	1/2 CUP	118.30 ML
1 1/4 TSP.	6.16 ML	1 CUP	236.59 ML
1 1/2 TSP.	7.39 ML	2 CUPS OR 1 PT.	473.13 ML
1 3/4 TSP.	8.63 ML	3 CUPS	709.77 ML
2 TSP.	9.86 ML	4 CUPS OR 1 QT.	946.35 ML
1 TBSP.	14.79 ML	4 QTS. OR 1 GAL.	3.79 L

Dry Ingredients

U.S. MEASURES		METRIC	U.S. MEASURES	METRIC
17 3/5 OZ.	1 LIVRE	500 G	2 OZ.	60 (56.6) G
16 OZ.	1 LB.	454 G	1 3/4 OZ.	50 G
8 7/8 OZ.		250 G	1 OZ.	30 (28.3) G
5 1/4 OZ.		150 G	7/8 OZ.	25 G
4 1/2 OZ.		125 G	3/4 OZ.	21 (21.3) G
4 OZ.		115 (113.2) G	1/2 OZ.	15 (14.2) G
3 1/2 OZ.		100 G	1/4 OZ.	7 (7.1) G
3 OZ.		85 (84.9) G	1/8 OZ.	3 1/2 (3.5) G
2 4/5 OZ.		80 G	1/16 OZ.	2 (1.8) G

INDEX

ACKNOWLEDGMENTS

I am grateful for the help of many people in making this book a reality, including everyone I've worked with at Sheraton Wild Horse Pass Resort & Spa, especially Kristen Jarnagin, Stephanie Heckathorne, Patrick Connors, Nicole Smith, and Ginger Sunbird Martin. Very special thanks to my co-authors and chefs Michael O'Dowd and Jack Strong, whose wonderful food inspired this book. Also thanks to Mason Malesevich, who manages Kai, and sommelier Lester Ilano for their help.

As a longtime fan of Arizona and especially the Phoenix area, my special thanks to Douglas MacKenzie of the Greater Phoenix Convention and Visitors Bureau, and many of his co-workers I have met along the way. Thanks also to Laura McMurchie of the Scottsdale Convention and Visitors Bureau, to Debra Utacias Krol of the Heard Museum, and to Chef Janos Wilder, proprietor and chef of Janos and J-Bar in Tucson and a member of the board of Native Seeds/ SEARCH.

I am also grateful for the talent and hard work of Ron Manville, for his superb food photographs, and to literary agent Nancy Love, and to editor Heather Carreiro at The Globe Pequot Press. —M.B.

Gratitude and thanks to the executive team at Sheraton Wild Horse Pass Resort & Spa and to the Gila River Indian Community for allowing me to cook and create from the heart, which not only flows like the river, but feeds my soul. It is the culinary team's effort and dedication in executing my vision that sustains us all. —M.O'D.

Thanks to the supportive and talented chefs I have worked with, who have helped me appreciate and love what we do. Special thanks to the tribal communities including my own, The Confederated Tribes of Siletz Indians, as well as the Gila River Indian Community. —J.S.

ABOUT THE AUTHORS

Marian Betancourt initiated and wrote *The Texas Hill Country Cookbook: A Taste of Provence* with Chef Scott Cohen. She is the author or coauthor of more than a dozen books and has written more than three dozen food articles for Associated Press Features. Her pieces on food and travel have also appeared in *Sante* magazine, *Irish America,* and *American Heritage,* where she wrote about the Pequot Mashantucket Indians of Connecticut. She has written about many well-known chefs, including Daniel Boulud, Bobby Flay, Tom Douglas, Michael Lomonaco, and David Rosengarten. She lives in New York City.

Michael O'Dowd, the award-winning Executive Chef of Wild Horse Pass Resort & Spa, is devoted to putting a contemporary spin on classical culinary methods with unique plate presentations emphasizing not only freshness and taste, but artful arrangement. With his extensive working knowledge of cuisine from Catalan to Native American, this chef relishes the challenge of creating what he terms "Native American Cuisine with Global Accents," which has earned Kai AAA Five Diamonds and Mobil Five Star awards. Previously Chef O'Dowd worked in the finest restaurants in New York as well as prestigious hotels such as The Ritz Carlton, and he has shared the kitchen with

Michael O'Dowd

Michelin Chefs Gunter Seeger, Boris Keller, and Pierre Orsi. He has been featured widely in the national food and beverage media, and appeared on David Letterman's opening television show. (O'Dowd's other passion is his racecar, which was featured in *Modified Luxury and Exotics.*)

Jack Strong, Chef de Cuisine, brings a rare combination of Native American heritage and luxury culinary experience to Kai. He has an extensive background incorporating locally grown and indigenous ingredients into high-end and specialty menus. Chef Strong is from the Confederated Tribes of Siletz Indians in Oregon and has a long history of using his culinary skills for community involvement. Before coming to Kai, Chef Strong was the sous chef at The Phoenician's Windows on the Green Restaurant in Scottsdale. Working at Kai gives him the opportunity to fulfill his dream of furthering the advancement of Native American cuisine and giving back to the local native community through the resort's programs with Gila Crossing School.

Ron Manville's photographs appear in many award-winning cookbooks, including the IACP and James Beard Award winner Sherry Yard's *The Secrets of Baking.* His other cookbooks include Noel Cullen's *Elegant Irish Cooking* and Marcel Desaulniers's *Celebrate with Chocolate,* Dwayne Ridgeway's *Lasagna: The Art of Layered Cooking,* and Wolfgang Puck's *Wolfgang Makes It Easy.* He previously worked with Marian

Jack Strong

Betancourt on *The Texas Hill Country Cookbook: A Taste of Provence.* He lives in Nashville with his wife Christine (www.ronmanville.com).